BURT FRANKLIN: BIBLIOGRAPHY & REFERENCE SERIES 384
Selected Essays in History, Economics, & Social Science 201

THE CAMBRIDGE PRESS

The "Daye Press," believed to be the first printing press
used in English America; now in the possession of the
Vermont Historical Society, Montpelier, Vt.

THE CAMBRIDGE PRESS

1638–1692

A HISTORY OF THE FIRST PRINTING PRESS ESTABLISHED
IN ENGLISH AMERICA, TOGETHER WITH A
BIBLIOGRAPHICAL LIST OF THE
ISSUES OF THE PRESS

BY

ROBERT F. RODEN

BURT FRANKLIN
NEW YORK

Published by LENOX HILL Pub. & Dist. Co. (Burt Franklin)
235 East 44th St., New York, N.Y. 10017
Originally Published: 1905
Reprinted: 1970
Printed in the U.S.A.

S.B.N.: 8337-3041X
Library of Congress Card Catalog No.: 79-132817
Burt Franklin: Bibliography and Reference Series 384
Selected Essays in History, Economics, and Social Science 201

Reprinted from the original edition in the Wesleyan University Library.

DEDICATED TO

WILBERFORCE EAMES

BIBLIOGRAPHER AND LIBRARIAN

IN

GRATEFUL RECOGNITION OF NUMEROUS
BIBLIOGRAPHICAL COURTESIES
AND KINDNESSES

FOREWORD

I HAVE endeavored in this work to deal historically and bibliographically with the history of the first printing press established in English North America.

To the several important monographs of Dr. Samuel A. Green (who has written authoritatively about Cambridge imprints), I wish to acknowledge, most gratefully, my indebtedness. I also desire to thank Mr. Wilberforce Eames, of the Lenox Collection of the New York Public Library, for his extreme kindness and invaluable aid.

R. F. R.

New York City, August 28, 1905

CONTENTS

LIST OF ILLUSTRATIONS

THE CAMBRIDGE PRESS

I

THE BEGINNINGS OF THE PRESS

1638–1639

In the summer of 1638 "The John of London," bearing a printing press, a printer, and three pressmen, approached the shores of New England, and ended one of the most memorable of voyages. The printer was Stephen Daye, of London, known to-day as the prototypographer of British North America. Time has written his name in golden letters in bibliographical history, while it has obscured that of the owner of the press, Joseph Glover, of Sutton, in Surrey, England, the dissenting minister, whose generosity and loving labors are responsible for the foundation of American typography. During the voyage he "fell sick of a feaver and dyed," but his wife carried out his undertaking, settling at Cambridge, Mass., where, in the latter months of 1638 (in March, 1639, according to Winthrop), "a printing house was begun," the first issue of the press being "the freeman's oath," the next being "an almanack made for New England by Mr. Peirce, Mariner," while the third was "the psalmes newly turned into metre."

9

It was in this manner that Cambridge became the first home of printing in the English colonies of America, and it is a not uninteresting fact that religious enthusiasm was the principal factor in the foundation of the press, as it was in the establishment of the earliest press of North America, in the City of Mexico, where exactly one hundred years earlier Juan Pablos printed with the Spanish types of Jacobo Cromberger the "Breve y mas compendioso Doctrina Christiana en lengua Mexicana y Castellana." During the winter of 1533–4 Don Antonio de Mendoza and Fray Juan de Zumárraga, the Viceroy-elect and the Bishop-elect of New Spain, frequently conferred together in Spain, and decided upon the establishment of a printing press in Mexico. Accordingly, toward the beginning of 1536, Cromberger, a prominent printer of Seville, selected type and a press, and sent them to Vera Cruz in the Spring, Juan Pablos (or Paoli), of Brescia, in Lombardy, accompanying the outfit as his representative. A century later Joseph Glover, Rector of Sutton, in Surrey, England, left the flock to whom he had preached for eight years, tendering his resignation with the design of emigrating to New England and founding there a printing press. At his own expense he provided a font of type and procured funds from friends in England and Holland for a complete printing establishment, "£49 and something more" being donated by seven men whose names were collected by Leonard Hoar in 1674: Major Thomas Clarke, Captain James Oliver, Captain Allen, Captain Lake, Mr. Stoddard, Mr. Freake, and Mr. Hues. Little is known of the members of this generous group, but their names are worthy of remembrance.

Glover's next task was to find a printer, and in London, June 7, 1638, he made an agreement with Stephen Daye to take charge of the press, although its supervision was to remain in his own hands. A little later he set sail for New England, with his wife and family, together with Daye, Daye's family, and three assistants to work at the printing. According to Sibley, the ship's company also included Ezekiel Rogers, of Rowley, in Yorkshire, and a large number of his townspeople, who in 1639 commenced a new settlement in New England named Rowley. Glover's death on the voyage thither did not seriously delay the starting of the press. His widow, Elizabeth Harris, who was his second wife, succeeded to his interests, and with her children took up residence in Cambridge, where the press was set up in the house of Henry Dunster, the first president of Harvard University. Winthrop says that the first printing was done in March, 1639, but the time at which he was writing was some years after the actual date, and "The Freeman's Oath" and Peirce's "Almanack," which he mentions as the first two issues of the infant press, were perhaps printed in December of the previous year.

Somewhat earlier than this—October 10, 1638— Hugh Peters, teacher of the First Church in Salem, referred to the establishment of the press in a friendly letter written to Patrick Copland, sometime minister in Virginia and author of the rare "Virginia's God be Thanked: A Sermon of Thanksgiving," London,

1622, but at this time preaching in Bermuda. "Wee
have a printery here," he declares, by "here" mean-
ing Cambridge, "and thinke to goe to worke with
some speciall things, and if you have any thing you
may send it safely." One of the "speciall things" was
evidently the Psalms, then being "newly turned into
metre" by Richard Mather, John Eliot, and Thomas
Welde. Another contemporary account is given by
Edward Johnson (who came here in the fleet with
Winthrop in 1630) in his "History of New-England,
from the English planting in the yeere 1628 until the
yeere 1652," London, 1654: "This yeare [1638] the
reverend and judicious Jos. Glover undertook this long
voyage, being able both in person and estate for the
work he provided, for further completing the Colonies
in Church and Common-wealth-work, a Printer
which hath been very useful in many respects."
Nothing definite is known about the early history of
this "Printer," whose name was written by himself in
1638 as "Daye," and again in 1655 as "Day." Thomas
says that he served his apprenticeship to a London
printer, but there is no proof of this. He was not skilled
in the art of typography, and in the contract made
with Glover engaged himself to work in New England
at the trade which he was using in London—that of a
locksmith. He was then in his forty-fourth year,
having been born about 1594 (although the Dictionary
of National Biography says 1610), as he gave his age
as sixty-two in a disposition made in 1656. His family
consisted of his wife (who before her marriage was the
relict of Andrew Bordman, a baker in Cambridge,

England); two sons, Stephen and Matthew, and a stepson, William Bordman. His son Stephen died in December, 1639, about a year and a half after the press was set up in "our Cambridge," as Prince phrases it, while Matthew seems to have helped his father in the printing, finally taking charge of the press on the former's retirement in the latter part of 1646. There is no proof in support of the assertion that the elder Daye was a descendant of the celebrated London printer, John Day (1522–1584), whose name was variously written "Day," "Daye," and "Daie." It is rather a singular coincidence, however, that the printer of the first complete metrical version of the Psalms, in England as in New England, was a Day.

"The Freeman's Oath," the first issue of the press, was printed by Daye on a half sheet of small paper. No copy of it has survived the shocks of time, and the earliest contemporary reprint is dated 1647. This was the oath which every man over twenty years of age, and six months a householder, was obliged to take in order to become a freeman of the Corporation, or a legal citizen of the Massachusetts Bay Company. The original draft, in the autograph of John Winthrop, is in the possession of the Boston Public Library. That "The Freeman's Oath" has been preserved to us is due to a quarrel in Massachusetts Bay between William Vassall, one of the richest settlers in the colony, and Edward Winslow, who had succeeded Bradford as governor in 1633. Although Vassall was a public-spirited man, his usefulness was considerably restricted by his inability to agree with those around him, and in 1646, with several equally discontented friends, he sailed for England to make his grievances known. Winslow had just published in London his "Hypocrisie Unmasked," and Vassall, using the name of "Major John Child," replied in 1647 in a pungent production, called "New-Englands Jonas Cast up at London: Or, A Relation of the Proceedings of the Court at Boston in New-England against divers honest and godly persons," in which he assailed Winslow's championship of New England's religious policy. Winslow speedily retorted with "New England's Salamander discovered by an irreligious and scornefull Pamphlet, called New-England's Jonas cast up at London," but the details of the controversy do not especially interest us. Our immediate concern is with Vassall's "New-Englands Jonas," one of the most important of books in relation to the first printing in Cambridge. The preface contains a statement regarding two of the seven lost issues of the Cambridge Press, which should be considered authoritative and final, the author referring the reader to: "the Capitol Laws of the Massachusetts Bay, with the Free-man's Oath, as they are printed there [Cambridge] by themselves;" and on page nine he reprints, presumably from his own copy:

"THE OATH OF A FREE-MAN.

"I (A. B.) being by Gods providence, an Inhabitant and Freeman, within the Jurisdiction of this Commonwealth; do freely acknowledge my self to be subject to the Government thereof: And therefore do here

14

swear by the great and dreadful Name of the Ever-living God, that I will be true and faithful to the same, and will ac-cordingly yield assistance & support there-unto, with my person and estate, as in equity I am bound; and will also truly endeavor to maintain and preserve all the liberties and priviledges thereof, sub-mitting my self to the whole-some Lawes & Orders made and established by the same. And further, that I will not plot or practice any evil against it, or con-sent to any that shall do so; but will timely discover and reveal the same to lawfull Authority now here established, for the speedy preventing thereof.

"Moreover, I doe solemnly bind my self in the sight of God, when I shal be called to give my voyce touch-ing any such matter of this State, in which Free-men are to deal, I will give my vote and suffrage as I shall judge in mine own conscience may best conduce and tend to the publike weal of the body, without respect of persons, or favour of any man. So help me God in the Lord Jesus Christ."

In spite of the extraordinary interest which attaches to the earliest extant specimens of the first few years of the Cambridge Press, — "The Bay Psalm Book," the Harvard Theses of 1643, the "Narrowgansets Declaration," etc., — "The Freeman's Oath," had it been preserved to our time in its original edition, would not be equalled by any of them as an important document in the early history of printing. It was, it is true, a mere broadside, and not a book, but although the first "Bay Psalm Book" is widely regarded as one of the most valuable examples of the world's incu-nabula, it is not to be questioned, we think, that a copy of "The Freeman's Oath" would sell higher to-day in the open market.

What, then, shall we say of Peirce's "Almanack" of 1639, the second issue of the press and the *first* English book printed in America? It is the custom of some bibliographical writers to refer to this almanac as a *pamphlet*, and to "The Whole Booke of Psalmes" of 1640 as a *book*, in very much the same way that they describe Atkins's "Kalendarium Pennsilvaniense" and Budd's "Good Order Established in Pennsilvania," Philadelphia, 1685, the first two issues of Bradford's press in America, and the first two works printed in English anywhere south of Massachusetts. But the terms, to my mind, are interchangeable, and the almanac of 1639 is unrivalled by "The Bay Psalm Book" and possesses a high and unassailable importance.

Encyclopædic in information, voluminous in bulk, moderate in price, the modern American almanac yearly makes its appearance. The earliest American almanac was a more primitive composition, although its audience, no doubt, was not without appreciation. Its edition was probably not small, but its ephemeral character was such that no copy is now known. Its author, referred to in Governor Winthrop's diary as "William Peirce, Mariner," was Captain William Peirce, born in England about 1590, and for a long period the most noted sailmaster that came into the New England waters. One of the most esteemed and accomplished navigators of his time, master of three of the five ships that brought the first settlers to New

England, and an intimate of Bradford, Winslow, and Winthrop, Peirce, in Mr. Littlefield's words, is "known to-day only as the compiler of an almanac."

That almanac, however, was the very beginning of printed literature in America. Thenceforward, scarcely a year passed over the first printing house in the Anglo-American colonies without a similar work coming from its lonely press. It has been stated that from 1639 until Matthew Day's death, ten years later, and the coming of Samuel Green, the third printer, an almanac for each year was printed in the same office; but the earliest extant example is the one for 1646, now represented by the solitary specimen, imperfect at the beginning and end, which rests in a private library in New York City. It is not known that Captain Peirce followed his pioneer almanac with others for 1640, 1641, 1642, 1643, 1644, and 1645, although it is quite possible. No writer or diarist of the period has chronicled their appearance, and if they were printed, they are wholly lost to this generation.

II

"THE BAY PSALM BOOK"

1640

ALTHOUGH we possess accidental proof that there were two issues of the Cambridge Press before 1640, "The Whole Booke of Psalmes," published in that year, is the oldest book which yields evidence of any kind concerning the first appearance of the typographical art in English America. That evidence is hardly satisfactory, the title-page concluding with the brief statement, "Imprinted 1640"; but despite the absence of the printer's name, the place of printing, and the names of its compilers, its high rank in the department of American incunabula is unassailable. Although it is not the rarest, it is the most coveted treasure of our first press, and should have far more interest for an American collector than a Caxton. As it is represented to-day by only four perfect copies, it shares the rarity of many of the achievements of England's first printer, and is justly classed with the Old World's most precious books. Whether one considers it from the bibliographical or historical viewpoint, its importance is great and lasting.

The typographical labor of the book was probably begun in 1639. The exact date is not known, but it

18

was, of course, anterior to 1640, the year of its publication. Daye is not supposed to have been a learned typographer, his workmen were untrained, his types were poor; the operations of the press, therefore, were slow. The result of his labors was a rudely printed quarto of 148 leaves, or 37 sheets, beginning with the title-page, within an ornamental type border, which is followed by a long preface of a little over twelve pages, the text, "The Psalmes in Metre," and a leaf, blank on the reverse, and containing on the recto a list of "Faults escaped in printing," which is briefer than it should be. The text ends with the fourth line on the reverse of the next to the last leaf, the remainder of the page being occupied with this "Admonition to the Reader:" "The verses of these psalmes may be reduced to six kindes, the first wherof may be sung in very neere fourty common tunes; as they are collected, out of our chief musicians, by Tho. Ravenscroft."
The chief compiler and editor of the book took pains, as we shall see, to excuse the weakness of the poetical translation; the printer did not attempt to explain the poorness of the press work. According to Isaiah Thomas, the type which he used was "Roman, of a size of small bodied English." In addition, a few words in Hebrew letters are employed in the preface, and may have been specially cut on wood or metal for this book. Typographical errors and curiosities of spacing exist throughout the book. Oddly enough, the heading at the top of each left-hand page is printed "Psalm," while on the opposite page the word

is spelled and spaced "Ps-alme." This, however, is
not the place in which to criticize the printer or the
printing; "The Whole Booke of Psalmes" is no less
a treasure despite its lack of typographical accuracy;
we are fortunate to possess it in any form, and can
but share the admiration of Thomas Prince,—the first
American who loved and collected American books,
—who always reverently prized and fondly regarded
this historically important work, printed at "our
Cambridge."

The work of translation from the original Hebrew
was begun as early as 1636. Cotton Mather, in his
"Magnalia," says that "the New-English reformers,
considering that their churches enjoyed the other ordinances of Heaven in their scriptural purity, were
willing that the ordinance of 'The singing of psalms,'
should be restored among them unto a share in that
purity." A new version was determined upon, and
"the chief divines in the country took each of them
a portion to be translated." The men most conspic-
uous in the sacred task were Richard Mather, of Dorchester, the progenitor of all the Mathers in New
England; John Eliot, of Roxbury, later to become
famous in history as the "Indian Apostle;" and
Thomas Welde (or Wells), pastor of the First Church
in Roxbury, where Eliot was associated with him as
"teacher." These men were divines, not poets.
Neither of them was a George Sandys, capable of
writing smooth, clear, and vigorous verse. Their
scriptural paraphrases are, in consequence, appall-
ingly tame. Wherever the original is peculiarly

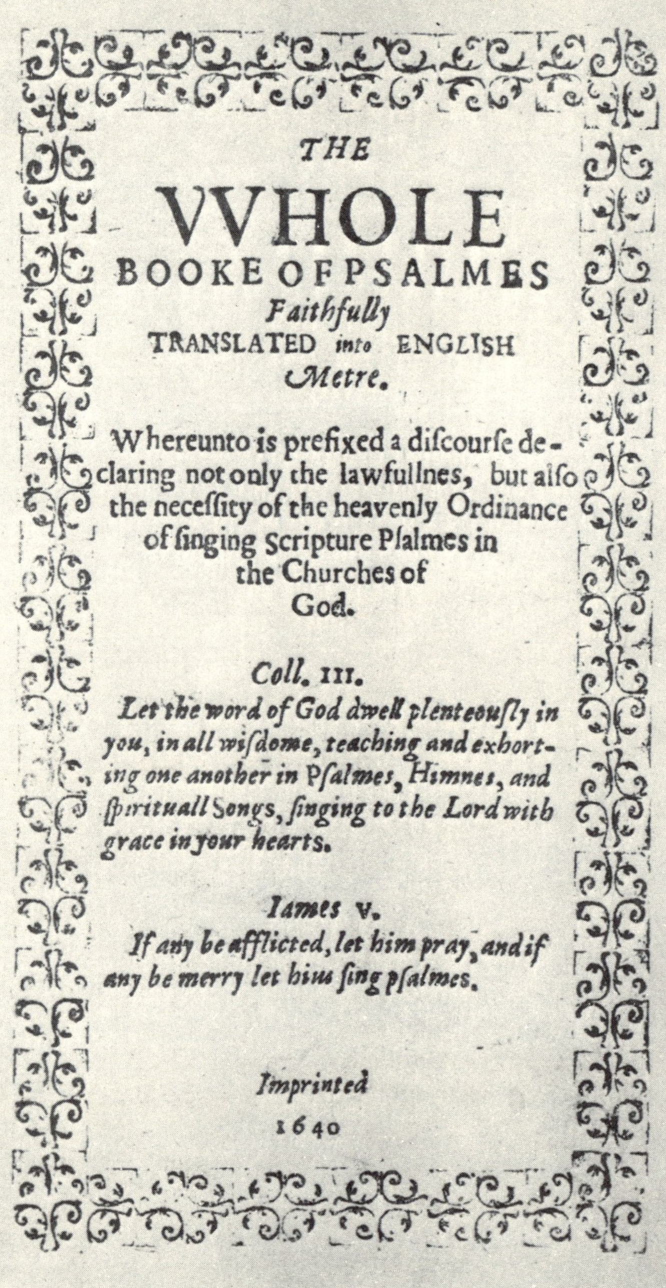

The Bay Psalm Book. 1640

striking, the New England version is singularly disappointing. Here is an example, from the 1st Psalm:

> O Blessed man, that in th' advice
>   Of wicked doeth not walk:
> nor stand in sinners way, nor sit
>   in chayre of scornfull folk.
> 2 But in the law of Iehovah,
>   is his longing delight:
> and his law doth meditate,
>   by day and eke by night.
> 3 And he shall be like a tree
>   planted by water-rivers:
> that in his season yields his fruit,
>   and his leafe never withers.
> 4 And all he doth, shall prosper well,
>   the wicked are not so:
> but they are like unto the chaffe,
>   which winde drives to and fro.
> 5 Therefore shall not ungodly men,
>   rise to stand in the doome:
> nor shall the sinners with the just,
>   in their assemblie come.
> 6 For of the righteous men, the Lord
>   acknowledgeth the way:
> but the way of ungodly men,
>   shall utterly decay.

Six of the Psalms are said to have been translated by Francis Quarles, the English poet, author of the now neglected "Sions Elegies," "Sions Sonnets," "Divine Fancies," "Divine Poems," etc. Holland, in his "Psalmists of Britain," 1843, says: "I regret that I can only incidentally introduce the name of Quarles into this volume: the general terseness of his style entitles us to believe that a Psalm from his pen could not have been without merit." John Josselyn, who came here in 1638, and again in 1663, publishing in 1674 "An Account of Two Voyages to New England," now prized among the minor Americana, tells us, however, that his friend Quarles gave him in 1638 metrical versions of six Psalms to take out to John Winthrop and John Cotton in America. These Psalms, intended for publication in "The Bay Psalm Book," and evidently printed as a part of that work, are, 16, 25, 51, 88, 113, and 137.

Professor Tyler has painted a vigorous and original word-picture of the poetical difficulties encountered by the principal translators in their pious labor, but our concern is not with the many marvels of metrical expression to be found in their book. It was compiled to serve a purpose, and it served that purpose well. The preface was written by Richard Mather, to whom the Assembly of Churches, the first of the Puritan synods of New England, had assigned the duty of composing an introduction for the new psalter, in order to explain and commend the work which had been prepared in the place of Sternhold and Hopkins. This preface, which the late literary historian calls "a characteristic bit of Puritan prose, very Hebraic in learning, very heroic in conscientiousness, sharp and minute in opinion, and quaint in phrase," closes with the following words:

"If the verses are not always so smooth and elegant as some may desire or expect, let them consider that Gods Altar needs not pollishings: we have respected rather a plaine translation, than to smooth our verses with the sweetnes of any paraphrase, and soe have attended Conscience rather than Elegance, fidelity rather than poetry, in translating the hebrew words into english language, and Davids poetry into english meetre, that soe wee may sing in Sion the Lords songs of praise according to his own will, untill hee take us from hence, and wipe away all our teares, & bid us enter into our masters joye to sing eternall Hallelujahs."

This eloquent apology for the inadequacies of the translation is important in several ways. It is the earliest extant specimen of prose written and printed in New England —a fact generally overlooked. It is also the first work of Richard Mather printed in America, some years earlier than his "lesser" catechism, of which no copy has survived, and twelve years earlier than his "Summe of Certain Sermons upon Genes: 15.6," which was issued by Samuel Green during the fourth year of his management of the Cambridge Press. The original manuscript of the preface is in the Prince collection in the Boston Public Library.

Such was the manner of compilation and printing of "The Whole Booke of Psalmes," popularly known to-day as "The Bay Psalm Book" (from Massachusetts Bay), but in its time more properly called "The New England Psalm Book." The edition consisted of seventeen hundred copies. The book was sold in all probability at the office of the press, and also in the shop of Hezekiah Usher, the earliest bookseller in New England, who was located at that time in

Cambridge. In 1640, the year of its issue, New England had twelve independent groups of colonists, fifty towns, and a total population of about 25,000. The audience to which the book appealed was large, therefore, and although a second edition was not called for until 1647, it is hardly possible that more than a few copies of the original issue then remained. Only ten copies are now in existence, of which five were once in Thomas Prince's noble "New England Library," now living a mere shadow of its former splendid self and including but two of the five examples, and those two, alas, imperfect!

The history of the ten existing copies has been variously told by various writers, and nearly always inadequately or inaccurately. Their individual history is as follows:

1. Perfect copy in the Bodleian Library, Oxford. This example, bequeathed to the Library in 1735 with Bishop Tanner's books, remained there unrecognized for over a century, the printed catalogue of sixty years ago recording its title without distinction among the ordinary editions of the Psalms in verse. Earlier in the Nineteenth Century it was seen by the Rev. Henry Cotton, who published in 1821 "A List of Editions of the Bible and Parts Thereof in English, from the Year MDV. to MDCCCXX," but although he had carefully examined the book and quotes from the preface and the text, it is dismissed on page 67 with this description: "1640. Psalms, in metre anonymous; no place, no name. 4to. Bodleian." After the unearthing in 1855 by Henry Stevens of the

copy now in the New York Public Library (Lenox collection), the librarian, in Stevens's words, became aware that he was "entertaining unawares this angel of the New World," and in 1877 it was exhibited, under its rightful colors, at the Caxton celebration. It is the only copy known in Europe.

2. Perfect copy in the New York Public Library (Lenox collection). This excellent copy, by reason of the seventh chapter of Henry Stevens's fascinating "Recollections of Mr. James Lenox and the Formation of his Library," 1886, is probably the best known of the extant examples. Stevens, who had long endeavored to obtain a copy for Mr. Lenox, finally came upon the "long lost Benjamin, clean, and unspotted," in Sotheby's auction rooms, January 12, 1855, at one of the sales of William Pickering's stock. It was unmentioned in the catalogue, being placed with a miscellaneous lot described as "Psalmes, other editions, 1630 to 1675, a parcel." The parcel was purchased by Stevens for nineteen shillings, the real character of its most important portion being unknown to the other buyers present. On collation, he missed "sundry of the Psalms, enough to fill four leaves," but knowing that an imperfect copy was in the possession of George Livermore, the American collector, he " proposed an advantageous exchange, and obtained the missing four leaves." Having thus completed his copy, he had it bound by Francis Bedford in red morocco, and sold it to Mr. Lenox for £80. This is the late bibliographer's account of the transaction. It is not entirely accurate, as the missing leaves, in reality, were twelve in number

—the whole of signatures W, X, and Y. The Livermore copy, once Prince's, was smaller than the copy discovered in London, and the supplied leaves were remargined while the volume was in Bedford's hands. The book is otherwise in fine condition, and is one of the glories of the great collection formed by the munificent New York bibliophile. In relation to this copy, a curious error has crept into one of the more recent accounts of the exchange with Livermore, George E. Littlefield, in his "Early Boston Booksellers, 1642 to 1711," saying: "Mr. Stevens proposed an exchange, agreeing to give Mr. Livermore certain pamphlets which he had previously offered to him, in return for the missing leaves. When Mr. Livermore came to examine the pamphlets, he discovered that one of them was the long sought for 'Souldier's Pocket Bible,' which had escaped the recognition of Mr. Stevens. He immediately informed him of his discovery, and it is unnecessary to say that Mr. Stevens was quite mortified over his slip." Quite different is the real history of this especial copy of "The Souldier's Pocket Bible," now in the New York Public Library, (Lenox collection), the only other example being in the British Museum, as it was presented to Mr. Livermore by a friend, the fly leaf saying: "George Livermore, Esq., with the regards of Edward A. Crowninshield." Henry Stevens, of Vermont and London, was too adroit and experienced a book-hunter to make serious mistakes.

3. Perfect copy in the John Carter Brown Library, Providence, R. I. This is the most interesting of all

existing copies of "The Bay Psalm Book"—a book
with a history and a provenance of distinction, ennobled and dignified by a long line of illustrious
possessors. It was first owned by Richard Mather, and
bears his autograph in several places, declaring it to be
"His Booke." Only a portion—an unimportant
portion—now remains of the Mather library, which
the lively Dunton called "the glory of New England,
if not of all America," Cotton Mather, who added to
it largely, calling it "Ye Darling of my Little Enjoy-
ments." The Mather collection passed to Increase
Mather, then to his son, Cotton Mather, and then to
the latter's son, Samuel. In 1775 most of the library
was destroyed by the fire that laid waste Charlestown,
regarding which John Adams wrote that "the loss of
Mr. Mather's library, which was a collection made by
himself, his father, his grandfather, and great grandfather, and was really very curious and valuable, is
irreparable." Long before 1775 this precious book
became a part of Prince's "New England Library,"
the formation of which began in 1703, and bears his
book-plate on the reverse of the title-page. Time and
man have not been reverent to the Prince collection,
which was left, by his will, to the Old South Church
(of which he was pastor for forty years,), to be deposited in the steeple chamber. The ravages of after
years, the vandalism of British troops: all served to
deplete the library, but the book-borrower and the
book-exchanger of the succeeding century wrought
irremediable ruin. Among the "book-exchangers"
were Nathaniel B. Shurtleff, Edward A. Crownin-

shield, and George Livermore, who in 1850 obtained
from the Committee of the Old South a number of notable items, among them being three copies of "The
Bay Psalm Book." These books are usually said to
have been procured "by way of exchange," which is
a convenient manner of dismissing a not overnice
transaction. As a matter of fact, the performance of
these gentlemen was not vastly different from that
of Thomas Frognall Dibdin, who in 1811 persuaded
the Dean and Chapter of Lincoln's Cathedral to let
him purchase certain highly valuable books at a very
inadequate price, some of which were immediately
resold at a very considerable advance to his patron,
Earl Spencer. The industrious Dibdin was audacious
enough to print a list of his acquisitions, which he
called "The Lincolne Nose-gay." The identity of
most of the Lincoln books has been lost or obscured,
but the Prince books can be traced to-day, although
the trio of New England bibliophiles, who followed
Dibdin's noble example, did not commemorate the
occasion with a privately issued "Nosegay" ("nose-
gay:" lit. "A pretty thing to smell"!). Into the hands
of the first-named of the trio passed the Mather copy
of the Psalm Book, and in 1862 a "literal reprint"
was made from it in Cambridge. Shurtleff (1810–1874),
antiquarian and politician, left behind a collection
that contained but one remarkable book — the one
now under discussion. His library was sold at auction
in Boston in November, 1875, but the Mather-Prince
"Bay Psalm Book" was withdrawn from the sale. A
year later it was again offered and was purchased by

a Providence book-seller for $1,025, which was then considered a high price, the British Museum having refused at £150 the Prince-Crowninshield copy, offered to the Keeper of Printed Books in 1860, and finally sold to George Brinley, of Hartford, Conn., for 150 guineas. Caleb Fiske Harris, of Providence, was the next owner, obtaining the book at private sale; and after his sudden death, in the Fall of 1881, it was again resold privately and passed into the John Carter Brown collection.

4. Perfect copy in the library of the late Cornelius Vanderbilt, New York City. This fine example was also in the Prince collection, but was allowed to pass, "by way of exchange," into the possession of Edward A. Crowninshield. The Crowninshield library, containing many of the rarest New England books, came upon the market after its owner's death, and was advertised to be sold at auction in Boston, November 1-4, 1859. It was disposed of privately to Henry Stevens, however, for a sum said to be $10,000. Stevens withdrew some of the best books, including the Prince copy of "The Bay Psalm Book," and sold the remainder at auction in London, July 12-20, 1860. As stated above, the British Museum authorities declined "The Bay Psalm Book" at Stevens's price of £150, as being too costly, with the consequence that England's national library still lacks this great treasure. The volume was placed in one of Bedford's handsomest bindings, — dark brown crushed levant morocco, — and in 1868 recrossed the Atlantic with Stevens, and was sold to the more appreciative Brin-

ley for 150 guineas. In March, 1879, the first part of the wonderful Brinley collection was sold in New York City, and this beautiful volume was bought by Cornelius Vanderbilt for only $1,200, the under-bidder, at $1,150, being a Chicago millionaire-bibliophile, who later regretted his loss of the book. Dr. James Hammond Trumbull, who edited the Brinley catalogue, described this invaluable volume in glowing words, saying that "The acquisition of a copy of the original edition of 'The Bay Psalm Book' must always be the crowning triumph to which every American collector aspires," and adding that "It is by no means probable that another copy will be offered for competition within the next quarter of a century." That prediction was not fulfilled, as the Prince-Livermore example was sold fifteen years later; but no *similar* copy has been offered. The Vanderbilt copy has been twice reported to have been destroyed by fire, but it still remains intact.

5. Slightly imperfect copy in the American portion of the Prince library, now deposited for all time in the Boston Public Library. A small part of a leaf in Ee is supplied in manuscript, but the volume is otherwise complete. It has the book-plate of "The New-England Library."

6. Slightly imperfect copy in the Prince collection, Boston Public Library. The last leaf of text (Ll 3) lacks a small portion, and the final leaf of the volume —"Faults escaped in printing"—is gone. The bookplate is not present.

7. Imperfect copy in the library of the American

Antiquarian Society, Worcester, Mass. The title-page is supplied in facsimile, and the last leaf is gone. This copy is interesting on account of its former ownership by Isaiah Thomas, the first historian of the American press. It bears his book-plate inside the front cover, and on a fly-leaf at the end is the following: "After advertising for another copy of this book, and making enquiry in many places in New-England &c I was not able to obtain or even to hear of another. This copy is therefore valuable, and must be preserved with the greatest care. It is in the original binding. I. T. Sept. 28th, 1820." This is evidently the copy referred to by Thomas in his "History of Printing in America," 1810, where he alludes to "An entire copy except title page, bound in parchment," which was then in "the possession of the Rev. Mr. Bentley of Salem."

8. Imperfect copy in the library of E. Dwight Church, Brooklyn, N. Y. The title-page, three following leaves, and the last three leaves at the end are supplied in facsimile. It bears the early autographs of John Dothirk, John Cotton, and Ann Dowding, and at a later period (1844) was owned by a member of the Shuttleworth family. In August, 1892, it was privately purchased in Boston by the late John Fletcher Hurst, Bishop of the Methodist Church, who resold it shortly before his death to Dodd, Mead, & Co., by whom it was advertised in April, 1903, at $4,000. Save for the imperfections noted, it is in clean, unwashed condition throughout, and is in the original (or contemporary) binding of sheep.

9. Imperfect copy in the library of Harvard University, Cambridge, Mass., presented to the library in 1764 by Middlecott Cooke, a graduate of the Class of 1723. The first six and the last three leaves are gone.

10. Imperfect copy in the library of A. T. White, Brooklyn, N. Y. This historically interesting example, formerly in the Prince collection, now lacks the title-page and eighteen other leaves, twelve of which, signatures W, X, and Y, were used by Henry Stevens to complete the copy now in the New York Public Library (Lenox collection). At one time in the Prince library it was acquired by the late George Livermore, and at his sale in Boston, November, 1894, was sold for $425.

III

FROM "THE BAY PSALM BOOK" TO THE FIRST NEW
ENGLAND CATECHISM

1641–1648

THE later history of the Daye press would puzzle the members of the positivist school of bibliography, who refuse to admit conjecture anywhere in the course of their researches. The press is supposed to have been very fruitful, but time has destroyed the majority of its productions, almost totally effacing, indeed, all evidence that they were ever printed. Of twelve works known to have been produced during the eight years that followed the issuing of "The Bay Psalm Book," only seven are now in existence: the Harvard Theses of 1643, the Narrowgansets pamphlet of 1645, the almanac of 1646, the almanac of 1647, the Theses of 1647, the 1647 edition of "The Bay Psalm Book," and the almanac of 1648. Five works have vanished: the Theses of 1642, the "Capitol Lawes" of 1643, the "Spelling Book" of 1644, the "Book of Laws and Liberties" of 1648, and Norris's Salem Catechism, also printed in or near 1648.

Other titles may be added to the five that have disappeared, but there is little certainty in the matter. One of the titles probably founded only on conjecture is the following, from Haven's list of "Ante-

Revolutionary Publications": "A Catechism agreed upon by the Elders at the Desire of the General Court. Cambridge, Daye, 1641." This was based on Winthrop's statement regarding the meeting of the General Court, in Boston, June, 1641, when it "was ordered that the elders should be desired to agree upon a form of catechism which might be put forth in print." This catechism, which was intended for "the instruction of youth in the grounds of religion," does not appear to have been printed. Wilberforce Eames does not believe that the elders ever agreed upon a uniform catechism, and Dr. Trumbull has said that "the early Congregationalists in New England did not object to *catechizing*, but had some difference of opinion about *catechisms;* and, moreover, regarded the catechetical instruction of the young as a duty of the *household*, rather than a distinct office of the church."

Stephen Daye's first typographical venture after "The Bay Psalm Book" is therefore unknown to us. In the autumn of 1642 he printed a broadside list of Theses at the Commencement of Harvard College, which is not now extant, the earliest contemporary edition being the reprint in "New England's First Fruits," London, 1643, the first of the Eliot Indian tracts. In the latter work is given, from a copy of the original: "A Copie of the Questions given and maintained by the Commencers in their publick Acts, printed in Cambridge in New-England, and reprinted here verbatim." Governor Hutchinson, in his "History of the Colony of Massachusetts Bay," reprints in the appendix to the first volume the Theses of 1642, saying that they were "published with a particular account of the whole proceedings in England. I know of but two copies extant." His reference was undoubtedly to the Indian tract, as he does not seem to have seen a copy of the original impression.

The first Commencement at Harvard was held in September, 1642, and "New England's First Fruits" was evidently written within a few weeks of the time when the first class was graduated. The first part of the tract gives an account of the earliest attempts to civilize and convert the Massachusetts Indians; the second part treats of "the progresse of learning in the colledge at Cambridge in Massachusetts Bay." The Theses of 1642, fortunately preserved in this precious pamphlet, gives the names of the members of the first class, "that remarkable group of young men whom Harvard sent forth in 1642, as the first specimens of high culture achieved in the woods of America:" Benjamin Woodbridge (1622–1684); George Downing (1623–1684), nephew of Governor Winthrop, and later renowned as soldier and politician; William Hubbard (1621–1704), clergyman and historian; Samuel Bellingham; John Wilson (1621–1691); Henry Saltonstall; Tobias Barnard; Nathaniel Brewster (1620–1690); and John Bulkeley (1619–1689).

Daye's next production was very possibly the "Capitol Lawes" of 1641 and 1642, which came from the press in 1643. This is one of the lost books, but the Cambridge edition is referred to in the preface of Vassall's "New England's Jonas Cast up at London," London, 1647, and the laws are quoted from in the body of the work. The General Court ordered the laws to be printed in the third month of 1643. Later in the year Daye printed the Theses of the second graduating class at Harvard, of which a solitary copy has come down to our time—the slightly imperfect example owned by the Massachusetts Historical Society, defective in the centre and at the right and left sides, but only lacking about ten words. This was also issued in broadside form. It gives the names of four graduates: John Jones; Samuel Mather (1626–1671); Samuel Danforth (1626–1674); and John Allin (1623— ?). This Samuel Mather, later a minister in Dublin, was the son of Richard Mather, and the author of a Cambridge book—"A Testimony from the Scripture against Idolatry & Superstition"— printed in 1670 by Green. Samuel Danforth was the Roxbury divine, whose almanacs for 1646, 1647, 1648, and 1649 are among the most prized examples of the incunabula of the Anglo-American press. The Theses of 1643—the second extant production of the Cambridge Press—was discovered in 1860 in one of the cabinets of the Massachusetts Historical Society, the librarian finding both it and the Theses of 1670 (printed by Green) in a small bundle of ancient papers in type and manuscript.

Another of the lost issues of the press is the "Spelling Book," about 1644, the title of which is given in a memorandum of seven books printed at Cambridge between 1639 and 1648, now preserved among the Dunster manuscripts in the archives of Harvard University. An Election sermon by Richard Mather and an artillery sermon by John Norton, each delivered in 1644, were ordered to be printed; but their titles cannot be added with authority to the brief list of early Cambridge imprints. According to the Massachusetts Records, the General Court ordered that "the printer shall have leave to print the election sermon, wth Mr. Mathews consent, & the artillery sermon, wth Mr. Nortons consent;" but there is no contemporary evidence that they ever existed. If Mather's discourse had been issued, it would have been the first Massachusetts Election sermon which was printed, preceding by nineteen years John Higginson's "Cause of God and his People in New-England, as it was Stated and Discussed in a Sermon Preached before the Honourable General Court of the Massachusets Colony, on the 27 day of May 1663, Being the Day of Election at Boston," which has long been famous as the earliest printed example of that memorable series of annual addresses. Cotton Mather does not seem to have known of the printing of his grandfather's discourse of 1644, as he declares, in his funeral address on Higginson, that "The Cause of God and his People in New-England" is "the First Born by the way of the Press, of all the Election Sermons that we have in our Libraries."

The next year witnessed the birth of the Narrowgansets book—now the third extant issue of the press and its earliest production possessing historical interest: "A Declaration of Former Passages and Proceedings betwixt the English and the Narrowgansets, with their confederates, Wherin the grounds and justice of

the ensuing warre are opened and cleared. Published,
by order of the Commissioners for the united Colonies: At Boston the 11 of the sixth month 1645."
This seven page quarto declaration of war against the
Narrowgansets, printed by Stephen Daye during the
summer of 1645, is signed by "Jo: Winthrop President,
In the name of all the Commissioners." The following entry, in "An account of Expences layed out for
ye country from August 1645 untill this 8th of October
1646," signed by President Dunster of Harvard and
preserved at the State House, shows the number of
copies printed: "First for ye printing five hundred
Declarations—4—00—00." The pamphlet was so rare
in Governor Hutchinson's time that he reprinted it,
in his "Collection of Papers," from a manuscript
copy, having "never met with it in print." Nevertheless, Winthrop's copy was in existence, and is now in
the library of the Massachusetts Historical Society,
indorsed in his handwriting: "Relation about Naro-
gansets & Miantinomo, and the discovery of their
plott agt. the English." A second copy was unearthed
in England by Henry Stevens in the middle '60's, but
was declined, at the reasonable price of ten guineas,
by both James Lenox and John Carter Brown. The
less capricious Brinley took it with eagerness in 1868,
and at his first sale, 1879, it went to the New York
collector who had previously refused it, costing him
$215, more than four times the original price, and is
now in the New York Public Library (Lenox collection).
Dr. Trumbull described it in the Brinley catalogue as
"probably unique," apparently not knowing of the

A DECLARATION OF FORMER

PASSAGES AND PROCEEDINGS BETWIXT THE ENGLISH
and the Narrowgansets, with their confederates, Wherin
the grounds and iustice of the ensuing warre are opened
and cleared.

*Published, by order of the Commissioners for the united Colonies:
At Boston the 11 of the sixth month
1645.*

THE most considerable part of the English Colonies professe
they came into these parts of the world with desire to advance
the kingdome of the Lord Jesus Christ, and to inioye his precious Ordinances with peace, and (to his praise they confesse) he hath not fail-
ed their expectation hitherto, they have found safety, warmth and refresh-
ing under his wing to the satisfaction of their soules. But they know, and
have considered that their Lord & master is King of righteousnes and peace,
that he gives answerable lawes, and casts his subjects into such a mould and
frame; that (in their weak measure) they may hold forth his virtues in their
course and carriage, not only with the nations of Europe, but with the barbarous natives of this wildernes. And accordingly both in their treaties &
converse they have had an awfull respect to divine rules, endeavouring to
walk uprightly and inoffensively, & in the midst of many injuries and inso-
lencies to exercise much patience and long-suffering towards them.

The Pequots grew to an excesse of violence and outrage, and proudly
turned aside from all wayes of justice & peace, before the sword was drawn
or any hostile attempts made against them. During those warrs, & after
the Pequots were subdued, the English Colonies were carefull to continue
and establish peace with the rest of the Indians, both for the present & for
posterity, as by several treaties with the Narrowganset & Mohiggin Saga-
mores may appeare: which treaties for a while were in some good measure
duly observed by all the Indians, but of late the Narrowgansets & especialy
the Niantceks their confederates have many wayes injuriously broke & vio-
lated the same by entertaining and keeping amongst them, not only many of
the Pequot nation, but such of them as have had their hands in the blood &
murder of the English, seizing and possessing at least a part of the Pequots
country

Winthrop copy. After the sale of Brinley's copy, a third example was obtained by the late Charles H. Kalbfleisch, and since his death has gone into another private collection. Dr. Green evidently refers to the Kalbfleisch copy when he declares that "two copies are in private hands:" his other example, the fourth now known, is undoubtedly owned in Boston. The John Carter Brown library is still without the little Indian book, once declined at ten guineas as being "too dear," but upon which we may now place a pecuniary value of at least three thousand dollars.

We come now to Samuel Danforth's "Almanack for the Year of our Lord 1646—" the earliest extant American almanac, represented by a unique copy, lacking the title-page, the second leaf, and the last leaf. Printed by Stephen Daye toward the end of 1645, it is apparently the last work issued during his management of the press, as his son Matthew seems to have succeeded him about a year later. The author was Samuel Danforth, whose name is given in the Harvard Theses of 1643 as the third member of the little class of that year. Born in Suffolk, England, in September, 1626, he came here at an early age. Thomas Welde, one of the compilers of "The Bay Psalm Book," and pastor of the First Church in Roxbury, went to England in August, 1641, as one of the agents of the colony, but although recalled in 1646, never returned. An assistant was needed to help Eliot, "whose Evangelical Employments abroad among the Indians, made a Collegue at Home to be necessary," and Danforth was chosen, his ordination taking place September 24, 1650. Here he remained until his death in 1674, neither "the Incompetency of the Salary," nor other inconveniences, being sufficient to "perswade him to remove unto more Comfortable Settlements." Much of his leisure time in early life was devoted to astronomical studies, and for several years he published almanacs,—1646 to 1649, inclusive,—in 1665 issuing "An Astronomical Description of the Late Comet as it Appeared in New England," and twenty-one years later a "New-England Almanack." Several specimens of poetry are to be found in his almanacs, the earliest of which now exist in unique copies. The chronological tables which they contain are valuable, and were consulted and cited by Thomas Prince in his "Chronological History of New England." The preservation of the almanacs is due to the interest taken in them by the Rev. Samuel Haugh, minister in Reading, Mass., whose signature appears on the title-page of the issue for 1649. At one time they were bound together (the almanac for 1650, by Urian Oakes, being included in the volume); and were interleaved and annotated by Haugh. They passed into the possession of Judge Sewall, the guardian of the clergyman's grandchildren, and remained in the Sewall family until their purchase by John K. Wiggin, of Boston, who sold them to George Brinley, of Hartford, for $1,000. Brinley broke the volume up, and at his first sale, 1879, the almanacs brought, respectively: 1646, $52.50; 1647, $80; 1648, $52.50; 1649, $45; and 1650, $52.50—a total of $282.50. The almanac for 1649, purchased for the Lenox library, is now in the New York Public Library. The almanacs for 1646, 1647, 1648, and 1650, purchased by the Hon. John Boyd Thacher, of Albany, N. Y., have recently been resold to Mr. E. Dwight Church, of Brooklyn, N. Y. The present valuation of the five almanacs, in the open market, would not be under $2500 each.

Danforth's almanac for 1647 is emphatically the most interesting production of the Daye press, bibliographically considered, as the title-page gives the place of printing, the printer's name, and the name of the earliest bookseller in English America: "MDCXLVII. An Almanack for the Year of our Lord 1647. Calculated for the Longitude of 315 degr. and Elevation of the Pole Arctick 42 degr. & 30 min. and may generally serve for the most part of New-England. By Samuel Danforth of Harvard Colledge Philomathemat. Cambridge Printed by Matthew Day. Are to be sold by Hez. Usher at Boston. 1647." Shortly before the production of this almanac, which was printed, perhaps, late in 1646, Stephen Daye is supposed to have resigned the management of the press, or to have been deposed because of trouble with President Dunster. The latter was then in practical charge of affairs, having become a partner in the management of the press by his marriage, June 21, 1641, with Mrs. Glover, taking complete control of the business after her death, August 23, 1643. After his withdrawal, the elder Daye seems to have resumed his former trade of locksmith, continuing at it until his death in December, 1668. His son, who succeeded him for a time as printer, was about twenty-six years of age when he produced the 1647 almanac. It will be observed that he gives his name in its imprint as "Day." It still remains a problem whether the family name was "Daye" or "Day."

Late in 1647 Matthew Day printed Danforth's "Almanack for the Year of our Lord 1648" ("Calculated" as in the almanac for 1647), although his name does not appear in the imprint, which is: "Printed at Cambridge. 1648." It was unquestionably his work, for the two almanacs, each of which has the title within a border made up of figures representing the phases of the moon, are exactly alike, typographically. These almanacs are printed in a much better manner than the one for 1646, issued by the elder Daye, and it is quite possible that the second Cambridge printer was provided with new fonts of type when Dunster gave him charge of the press. A few weeks before the issuing of the almanac for 1648, Matthew Day printed the list of Theses for 1647, in broadside form, similar to the list for 1643. The Massachusetts Historical Society has the only extant copy, and this is very defective, lacking the upper half. There were seven graduates this year, among them being Jonathan Mitchel (1624–1688); Nathaniel Mather (1630–1697), the son of Richard Mather; and William Mildmay, the son of Sir Henry Mildmay, of Essex, England, who was sent over, with Richard Lyon as tutor, to be educated at Harvard. Lyon, it is not uninteresting to note, resided in the house of President Dunster and assisted him in the revision of "The Bay Psalm

Book," printed in 1651 by the third Cambridge printer, Samuel Green.

Earlier in 1647 the second edition of "The Bay Psalm Book" came from the press of the younger Day. This was a reprint, without additions, of the first edition, although there were some changes in the spelling and punctuation. It is a small duodecimo. It was printed in a smaller type, and the general appearance is superior to that of the edition of 1640. The imprint is equally indefinite: "Imprinted 1647." Various opinions exist as to whether the printing was executed here or in England, but there is no good reason for the assigning of the book to a London press. Dr. Green, who declares that there is little evidence on which to base this conjecture, says: "After a comparison, side by side, with the Harvard list of Theses for 1647—which must have been printed here—I am inclined to think that the second edition of 'The Bay Psalm Book' came from Day's press."

Two copies are known of this second edition. One copy is in the British Museum, where it was long catalogued as follows: "Rous (Francis). Psalms, 1647," the cataloguer having evidently in mind Rouse's amended translation of the "Psalms, in Metre," printed in London in 1646. A second copy, discovered in England by Henry Stevens, was sold to George Brinley for £100, after James Lenox had refused it at that sum. At the first Brinley sale Caleb Fiske Harris paid $435 for it, and after Harris's death it passed into the John Carter Brown collection. This edition, it will be noticed, is much rarer than the first. The original impression was sold, no doubt, in Usher's shop in Boston.

Matthew Day's next undertaking was the "Book of Laws and Liberties," published by order of the General Court, and referred to in the "8th month, 1648," as "now at the Presse." This is still another of the lost books of the early Cambridge Press, the entire edition, which Whitmore says was extensive, having disappeared. Edward Norris's Salem Catechism, supposed to have been printed about this time, is also lost to us. This would appear to be the last of the younger Day's publications, as the press, in all probability, came under the control of Samuel Green late in 1648. He died in Cambridge, unmarried, May 10, 1649.

Norris's catechism is referred to by Cotton Mather in his "Magnalia." "Few Pastors of Mankind," he says, "ever took such pains at Catechising, as have been taken by our New-English Divines : Now let any Man living read the most judicious and elaborate Catechisms published, a lesser and a larger by Mr. Norton, a lesser and a larger by Mr. Mather, several by Mr. Cotton, one by Mr. Davenport, one by Mr. Stone, one by Mr. Norris, one by Mr. Noyes, one by Mr. Fisk, several by Mr. Eliot, one by Mr. Seaborn Cotton, a large one by Mr. Fitch; and say, whether true Divinity were ever better handled." In one of the Dunster manuscripts, which mentions seven books printed at the press between 1639 and 1648, is this entry: "In Norriss's Katechism about 3 Rheam Paper 7. 10. 00." The author of this vanished volume, Elder Edward Norris, was the associate of Hugh Peters in

the First Church in Salem in 1640, and had sole charge
of the church from 1641 to 1657. He came from England about 1639, and died in Salem in 1659. His little
book was the earliest printed New England catechism. Its disappearance is a real loss, but when we
reflect that the substantial "Book of Laws and Liberties" is not extant, we can easily conceive that such
an ephemeral publication as a catechism should not
survive.

The fate of the press used by Stephen and Matthew
Daye has been recently discussed by General Rush
C. Hawkins in two interesting papers, "The Daye
Press," (published in *The Literary Collector* December, 1903, and March, 1904). According to General
Hawkins, the pedigree of this press (now apparently
in the possession of the Vermont Historical Society)
"seems to go back in a fairly well connected chain
to the time of its being set up in Cambridge by
Stephen Daye." After Daye's time it was used, he
thinks, by Samuel Green, "who managed the business,
a part of the time with Marmaduke Johnson, until
near the end of the century." Green died in 1702,
and according to Isaiah Thomas's "History of Printing," "soon after his decease the printing materials
were removed from Cambridge, and probably sold."

At this sale, General Hawkins believes, the press
passed into the possession of Timothy Green, a descendant of Samuel Green, and also a printer, who in
1714 went from Boston and set up a printing establishment at New London, Connecticut, which he with
others of the Green family managed for more than a

century. About 1770, he states, two of their relatives, Judah Paddock Spooner and Alden Spooner, were apprenticed to the Greens. In 1773 they had learned enough of their art to become efficient workmen; for in that year they formed a partnership with the second or third Timothy Green and went with him to Norwich, Connecticut, where they opened a printing establishment in which they continued as partners until 1778, when the Spooners removed to the New Hampshire Grants, carrying with them the "Daye Press" as a part of their shop equipment. Upon this press the Spooners printed Aaron Hutchinson's rare Convention Sermon of 1777, "A well tempered Self-Love a Rule of Conduct towards others," (the first book printed in Vermont), and other important early Vermont imprints.

In support of this seemingly naked assertion about the transmigration of the "Daye Press," General Hawkins gives several printed statements "which in a court of antiquarians would be given credence and accepted for its face value." From the time of the two printers who thus removed the press the pedigree of this important typographical relic is complete down to the present day. After leaving the possession of the Spooners it passed through the hands of various printers in Vermont, was then consigned to the dust of sundry barns and lofts in Windsor County, Vermont, and finally, a few years ago, was secured by the newspaper men of that State and presented to the Vermont Historical Society, in whose rooms, in the State House at Montpelier, it found "a worthy resting place befitting its value as an item in the world of things that are curious and instructive."

As General Hawkins points out, the incredulous may still continue to ask where was the press after the death of Samuel Green in 1702 and up to the time of its appearance in Dresden, Vermont, in 1778, when the Spooners printed Hutchinson's Convention Sermon? Are we sure it is the Daye Press? These are the principal questions brought forward in his two papers, but although he answers them to his own satisfaction, it is impossible wholly to agree with his conclusions. General Hawkins seems to have forgotten that more than one press was used in Cambridge. The first press, the "Daye Press," was used by Stephen Daye, and by his son, Matthew, and then passed late in 1648 into the hands of Samuel Green, the third printer at the Cambridge Press. A second press was sent over in the autumn of 1659 by the Corporation for the Propagation of the Gospel Amongst the Indians in New England, in order that the publication of Eliot's Indian Bible, then ready for printing, might be hastened and aided. Marmaduke Johnson, who was sent from England in 1660 to assist Green, returned home at the end of the period for which he was engaged, but came back in the spring of 1665 with a new press. This press, which he operated for nearly ten years, was acquired at his death, in December, 1674, by John Foster, the first printer in Boston, and passes out of this discussion.

We have, then, two presses used in Cambridge by Stephen Daye, his son, Matthew, and by Samuel

Green, from the starting of printing there in the fall of 1638 to the publication of the second issue of Cotton Mather's "Ornaments for the Daughters of Zion," brought out in the early part of 1692. Which of the two is the "Daye Press"? One of Samuel Green's sons, Bartholomew, set up in the printing business in Boston early in 1690, but his shop was destroyed by fire shortly after and he was obliged to return to Cambridge, where he assisted his father until the closing of the press. In the spring of 1692 he returned to Boston, his father presenting him with a printing press and types, and was actively engaged as a printer until his death, in December, 1732. General Hawkins seems to be ignorant of these facts. It is possible that Samuel Green gave the earlier press (Daye's) to his son Bartholomew when he set up his first Boston press, and if this was the case it was destroyed by fire in 1690. It is also possible that the Daye Press was the one presented to Bartholomew Green by his father in 1692, and that the former, having procured a new press, gave the first Cambridge press to Timothy Green, when the latter went to New London, in 1714, to engage in the printing business. It is altogether probable that this is the true story of Timothy Green's acquisition of the "Daye Press," the most precious relic in the history of American typography, which now occupies a high and honored position among the treasures of the Vermont Historical Society.

IV

THE THIRD CAMBRIDGE PRINTER

1649–1650

SAMUEL GREEN (1615–1702), the third printer in Cambridge and the father of a race of printers, is supposed by most bibliographical writers to have assumed the management of the press in May, 1649, soon after the death of Matthew Day, the second printer. We may reasonably believe, however, that he began to print during the last days of 1648, issuing "An Almanack for the Year 1649. By Samuel Danforth," which differs, typographically, from Danforth's almanacs for 1647 and 1648, printed by the younger Daye, but agrees, in its make-up, with Urian Oakes's almanac for 1650, also printed by Green. Only one copy of his first imprint is now known,—the unique example in the New York Public Library (Lenox collection), formerly owned by "Sa: Haugh" (the Rev. Samuel Haugh), whose autograph it bears upon the title, later in the possession of Judge Sewall, and more recently in that of George Brinley.

Unlike Stephen Daye, the third Cambridge printer was not bred to the art, nor "especially acquainted with it," as Thomas said of John Foster. His earliest imprints, nevertheless, compare favorably with those

of the Dayes, father and son, and his later works,
however faulty, must be allowed to rank above the
productions of the first two printers at the press. His
first work, as we have seen, was issued about the end
of 1648, and from that time onward his labors were
incessant and rapid until his retirement in the early
part of 1692. Those labors were lessened in 1660 by
the coming of Marmaduke Johnson, a skilled typographer, sent from England to assist in the production
of Eliot's Indian Bible, the greatest achievement of the
Cambridge Press. Johnson's establishment, in 1665,
of a new press, was the first display of typographical
rivalry in New England; Foster's Boston press, started
in 1675, was a more serious rival; but these presses
rose and fell while he was still active, Johnson dying
in 1674 and Foster in 1681. In 1685, in Philadelphia,
with Bradford's printing of Atkins's "Kalendarium
Pennsilvaniense," came the establishment of the first
press in the middle Colonies. In 1692, one year before
the starting of Bradford's New York press, Samuel
Green ceased to operate his press, dying ten years
later at his home in Cambridge at the age of eighty-
seven. Although not the first printer at our first
press, his name and not that of Stephen Daye is the
most glorious name in its history. To him and not
to Daye—unduly honored in the annals of American
typography—properly belongs the title of " Our
Caxton."

Several of Green's earliest imprints, issued during
the first few months of his management of the press,
are doubtless lost to us; one imprint, assigned to

that period, was printed many years later in Boston by
his youngest son, Bartholomew. The latter possesses
this fascinating title : "Oratio Quam Comitijs Cantab-
brigiensibus Americanis Peroravit reverendissimus
D. D. Samuel Whiting Pastor Linnensis; in aula
scilicet Harvardina, Pridie Calendas Sextiles, Anno,
M.DC.XL.IX;" and at the first glance would seem to
be a Cambridge imprint of 1649. This Latin pamphlet
of sixteen pages, with no regular title-page, has been
included under that year in one list of New England
incunabula; but in Samuel Sewall's "Diary," under
the date of September 17, 1709, we read: "Mr. Green
[Bartholomew Green] finishes printing Mr. Whiting's Oration." Sewall, no doubt, had the original
manuscript of this oration, delivered at Harvard July
13, 1649, and this edition was privately made for
him.
The principal book issued by Green in 1649, and the
first important work of his press, was "A Platform
of Church-Discipline gathered out of the Word of
God: and agreed upon the Elders: and Messengers
of the Churches assembled in the Synod at Cambridge
in New England To be presented to the Churches
and Generall Court for their consideration and acceptance, in the Lord. The Eight Moneth Anno 1649.
Printed by S G at Cambridge in New England and
are to be sold at Cambridge and Boston Anno Dom:
1649." This was the first edition of the "Cambridge
Platform," the basis of New England theology, and
the first work with the imprint of Samuel Green. In
1645 the time had come when, as Cotton Mather says

in the "Magnalia," it was "convenient" that the Churches of New England should have "a System of their Discipline, extrated from the Word of God, and exhibited unto them, with a more effectual, acknowledged and established Recommendation: And nothing but a Council was proper to compose the System." In May, 1648, the Court passed an order expressing a "desire" that the Churches of Massachusetts send their elders and messengers to sit in Synod in Cambridge on the first day of September, "to discusse, dispute & cleare up, by the word of God," certain questions of church government and discipline. This Synod, "a grave, learned, and pious body," sat for two weeks, finally appointing John Cotton, of Boston; Richard Mather, of Roxbury; and Ralph Partridge, of Duxbury, to be each a committee of one to draw up the plan of a Scriptural model of church government, so that the three might be compared. Fifteen months later, when the three alternative schemes of congregational polity were submitted to the Synod, it was not Cotton's, as might have been expected, but Mather's platform which was adopted. Dr. Dexter calls it "a terse, clear, and well balanced summary of the general system which had been already outlined in the treatises of the New England elders; enlarged by being carried to its logical conclusions on a few points which had never been fully developed." Cotton's plan is not extant; Partridge's, lost long, was discovered by Dr. Dexter in 1873; Mather's draught is among the treasures of the American Antiquarian Society, together with the revised copy from which

A
PLATFORM OF
CHURCH DISCIPLINE

*GATHERED OUT OF THE WORD OF GOD:
AND AGREED UPON BY THE ELDERS:*
AND MESSENGERS OF THE CHURCHES
ASSEMBLED IN THE SYNOD AT CAMBRIDGE
IN NEW ENGLAND

To be prefented to the Churches and Generall Court
for their confideration and acceptance,
in the Lord.

The Eight Moneth   Anno 1649

Pfal: 84 1.   *How amiable are thy Tabernacles O Lord of Hofts?*
Pfal: 26 8.   *Lord I have loved the habitation of thy houfe & the
place where thine honour dwelleth.*
Pfal: 27.4.   *One thing have I defired of the Lord that will I feek
after, that I may dwell in the houfe of the Lord all the
dayes of my life to behold the Beauty of the Lord & to
inquire in his Temple.*

Printed by *S G* at *Cambridge* in *New England*
and are to be fold at *Cambridge* and *Boston*
Anno Dom: 1649.

A Platform of Church Discipline. 1649

the document as adopted by the Synod was printed by Green.

The "Cambridge Platform," issued by Green in the late summer of 1649, is a well-printed quarto, the platform itself occupying twenty-nine pages, prefaced by an introduction of ten pages, by Cotton, the latter being, so far as is known, the first of his works printed in New England. The edition, sold both in Green's office in Cambridge and in Usher's book-shop in Boston, must have been extensive; but the book is now, in Dr. Trumbull's words, "inexpressibly rare." The highest auction price is $210 (Brayton Ives sale, 1891); but this sum by no means represents the present value of a fine copy. Reprints of the book are numerous. The first English edition, full of errors, was issued in London in 1652: "London, Printed by William Bentley for John Ridley;" but although referred to by Edward Winslow in his preface to the London edition of the following year, has been practically unnoticed by the bibliographers. Kalbfleisch's copy, thought to be unique, was presented to the Lenox Library in 1898. An explanation of its rarity is given by Winslow in the second London edition, 1653: "Printed in New-England; and Reprinted in London for Peter Cole." Referring to the first English edition, he says: "Meeting with a Coppy thereof Reprinted, not only in a disorderly way, but very Falsly, to the great prejudice of the Work, I made it therefore my work to Suppress that Impression, and have gained a Promise, They shall never come to publick sale." The second American edition was printed at Cam-

bridge in 1671 by Marmaduke Johnson, the fourth
Cambridge printer; the third edition was printed in
Boston in 1680 by John Foster, by order of the
General Court. Another Boston edition, bearing the
date of 1701, was issued by Green's son, Bartholomew,
in conjunction with John Allen. The earliest edition
printed south of Massachusetts: "New York. Printed
by William and Andrew Bradford 1711," is one of the
very few and very rare volumes possessing the imprint
of the two Bradfords.

Late in 1649 there came from Green's press Urian
Oakes's "Almanack for the Year 1650," the first published work of "the Lactantius of New England." The
author's name does not appear upon the title-page,
and the imprint reads: "Printed at Cambridge 1650;"
but the little pamphlet, printed in the same style as
the almanac of 1649, is known to be Green's, and the
author was long since identified by Dr. Trumbull. The
almanac, calculated as in Danforth's almanacs for
1646, 1647, 1648, and 1649, bears upon the title-page
the Latin line: "Parvum parva decent, sed inest sua
Gratia parvis," the "apposite Verse" alluded to by
Cotton Mather in his sketch of Oakes: "A Lad of
small, as he never was of great Stature, he published a
little parcel of Astronomical Calculations." Misled by
Mather's reference, Thomas entered in his "History"
this title: "Astronomical Calculations. By a Youth.
(Urian Oakes), 1648, about," and said that it was not
known when or by whom it was printed, although
it was very possibly among Stephen Daye's productions. Oakes, born in England about 1631, and brought

over to New England by his parents while yet a child, had scarcely reached manhood when this almanac was published. He was a member of the graduating class at Harvard of 1649, and continued to reside at the college until 1653. No other work by him is known to have appeared until 1673, when Samuel Green printed his election sermon, "New England Pleaded with, And pressed to consider the things which concern her Peace." His almanac exists in the unique Haugh-Sewall-Brinley-Thacher copy, now in the Church collection. The latter is the last of the five Cambridge almanacs owned by the reverend antiquary of Reading, Mass., which, gathered at the time of issue, have been fortunately preserved to our day.

In the history of Green's press the year 1650 is a year of lost books. Two works may definitely be assigned to this year—Samuel Danforth's Roxbury Catechism and the Supplement to the law book of 1648–1649. To these we may add, perhaps, an almanac. In one of the Dunster manuscripts this entry appears: "Almanacks and Thesis 5 Years." The manuscript refers to the first five years of Green's occupancy of the press, and the inference is that an almanac and a list of theses were published each year. We have the almanacs for 1649 and 1650, but the other titles are utterly lost and unattainable. In the list of the earliest works of Green, "Mr. Danforth's Katechism" is placed between the "Sinod Books" [Cambridge Platform] of 1649 and "The Bay Psalm Book" of 1651. Wilberforce Eames, in his bibliographical account of "Early New England Catechisms," describes Danforth's book under Roxbury, stating that it was most likely printed in Cambridge not long after his ordination, September 24, 1650. No example of this catechism has been preserved, although one hundred copies are thought to have been printed.

Although the absence of Danforth's catechism and of the almanac of 1651 is to be regretted, their interest, at the most, was transient. The disappearance of the Supplement to the Code of Laws of 1648–1649, which was unquestionably printed in 1650, is a more serious loss. The "Body of Liberties," the first Code, was prepared in 1641 by the Rev. Nathaniel Ward, of Ipswich, the "Simple Cobbler," and, after revision, was adopted for three years by order of the General Court. It is believed to have been printed by Daye about 1643, but although there is contemporary evidence of its former existence, it is unknown to-day. The laws themselves can be traced, in slightly altered form, in the extant law book of 1660, where, although the first Code is not definitely cited, the majority of the sections have the dates of their enactment appended, enabling us to easily trace the laws assigned to 1641. Under the date of 1648 comes the first collection of the laws of the Colony, the chief inciter of the edition probably being Richard Bellingham. On May 10, 1648, the book of laws was "at press." October 27, 1648, the book was still "at the press," and the printing, perhaps, was not finished until the spring of the following year, formal sanction not being given until May, 1649, at the meeting of the General Court. We have thus, in Whitmore's words, "no official statement as to the month in which the completed volume was issued." If the book was not published until May, 1649, it is highly probable that Matthew Day was assisted in the printing by Samuel Green. The long delayed volume has vanished, in spite of the fact that an edition of six hundred copies was made. Fifty copies were given to the members of the Legislature, and the remainder were ordered to be sold at three shillings each. A certain portion of the edition was turned to waste paper or burnt—seventy copies or thereabouts.

We come now to the lost Supplement of 1650, printed by Green, and put through the press under the supervision of Joseph Hills (Member of the House for Charlestown in 1647 and Speaker in that year), who was its compiler. October 17, 1649, the following vote was passed by the General Court:

"The Court, finding by experience the great benefit that doth redound to the country by putting of the law in print, do conceive it very requisite that those laws that have passed the consent of the General Court since the Book of Laws were in printing or printed, should be forthwith committed to the press; and for that end appoint Richard Bellingham, esq., Mr. Nowell, Mr. Auditor-General [Duncan], Capt. Keayne, and Mr. Hills, or any three of them, a committee to prepare them against the Court of Election; that upon approbation of the return of the committee, they may also be printed; as also therewith to prepare those laws referred to in the end of the printed laws, with a suitable table, to be printed."

October 18, 1650, the General Court ordered that:
"Richard Bellingham, esq., the Secretary [Rawson], and Mr. Hills, or any two of them, are appointed a committee to take order for the printing the laws agreed upon to be printed, to determine of all things in reference thereunto, agreeing with the president for the printing of them with all expedition, and to allow the title if there be cause."

These entries positively determine the former existence of both the Code of 1648–1649 and of the supplementary laws of the following year. The late William Henry Whitmore, who unravelled the puzzling bibliography of the colonial laws, has enabled the student to form a satisfactory idea of the shape and contents of both of these. Citations given by him, under dates of May 26, 1652; August 30, 1653; May 3, 1654; and November 24, 1654, prove that the General Court in 1654 referred to and amended laws in the "first printed book" [the lost collection of 1648–1649] and in the "second printed book" [the lost Supplement of 1650]. Whitmore's description of the latter work, given in 1890 in his historical account of the printing of the New England laws, is the first mention made of it by any bibliographer. For two hundred and forty years it was an unknown work; the thirteen years which have elapsed since Whitmore's discovery have not witnessed the unearthing of a copy, and its title must be added to the long list of lost Cambridge imprints.

V

FROM THE REVISED "BAY PSALM BOOK" TO THE LAW BOOK OF 1660

1651–1660

In 1651 Green was chiefly busied with the production of one book, the only work which we may confidently assign to that year, although an almanac was perhaps printed during its closing months. But barren as the year appears to the unthinking, its solitary imprint is one of the glories of the Cambridge Press. Bearing the title of "The Psalms Hymns And Spiritual Songs Of the Old and New Testament, faithfully translated into English metre, For the use, edification, and comfort, of the Saints, in publick, & private, especially in New-England," this wonderfully precious book is valued to-day as the first edition of the revised version of "The Bay Psalm Book" and the earliest work containing the full name of the third Cambridge printer. Long thought to have disappeared, and now represented by one copy, this revision is the rarest of all extant editions of "The Bay Psalm Book;" with the one exception of the first edition of Eliot's Indian Bible, it is emphatically the chief production of Green's press.

Soon after the appearance of the second edition of the psalm book it was thought necessary to subject

the work to a thorough revision. This task was en-
trusted to the care of Henry Dunster, the first president
of Harvard and director of the press, and Richard
Lyon, who had come over from England as tutor
to William Mildmay, of the class of 1647. The preparation of the new edition is believed to have required
the labor of about three years. The editors performed
their task with thoroughness, and their revised
and improved version was reprinted in many editions
without further alteration until 1758, when the Rev.
Thomas Prince attempted to improve it "by an endeavour after a yet nearer approach to the inspired
original, as well as to the rules of poetry." The
editors of 1651 declared that they had translated the
Psalms, "with speciall care & diligence into such
Meeters as are most usuall and suitable for such holy
poems," having a special eye "both to the gravity of
the phrase of Sacred writt, and sweetnes of the
verse." Their revision was the first to contain the
Spiritual Songs, which were added by Lyon.

Green, who issued the new "Bay Psalm Book" in a
small octavo volume of 381 pages, printed an extensive
edition, putting forth as many as two thousand copies.
Despite the size of the edition, copies were unknown
to Thomas when he compiled his "History." He
mentions a somewhat similar title, but describes the
book as "crown 8vo, 308 pages," and places it under
the year 1650. The bibliographers and literary histo-
rians of the past blindly followed Thomas; their
successors of to-day likewise err, although the book
is accurately described in the sixteenth volume of

Sabin's "Dictionary of Books Relating to America,"
a not inaccessible work. In 1886, when Mr. Eames
gave for the first time a bibliographical description of
Dunster and Lyon's revision, the only known copy was
in "the unrivalled collection of Mr. C. H. Kalbfleisch."
In 1898, some few years after Mr. Kalbfleisch's death,
this copy privately passed, together with other of the
Kalbfleisch rarities, into the possession of the New
York Public Library (Lenox collection). It was then
believed to be unique, and still possesses that distinction.

For over a decade this little book, boasting an
attractive contemporary binding, and in beautiful,
original, unsophisticated condition from beginning to
end, has been famous among collectors of American
incunabula. Mr. Kalbfleisch is supposed to have
procured it from Henry Stevens in the early '80's at
a cost of $1,000. Its pedigree, unfortunately, has been
imperfectly preserved. The second fly-leaf bears the
signature of "Robert Wright 14th April. 1836," and on
the back of the title-page is this line: "Robert Wright
bought this book in 1836." Its original owner seems
to have been the "F. B.," whose initials appear in
gold letters upon the sides. His identity is unknown
to us, and has not been determined by research. The
book was possibly bound for him during the third
quarter of the seventeenth century by Edmund
Ranger, of Boston, who was bookbinder as well as
bookseller, and "the only man of his calling whose
name has come down to us from that particular
period." The binding strongly appealed to William

Loring Andrews, who mentioned it with special observance in his "Bibliopegy in the United States and Kindred Subjects," 1902. "Well and stoutly bound in brown calf," he wrote, "its covers are held together by leathern and brass clasps, the only attempt at ornamentation being a narrow gold line traced around the borders of each side, a small centre ornament, and the initials F. B. If it is, as we presume, the original binding, it is one of the earliest examples extant of bookbinding executed in North America, for the old Bay State may pride itself upon having been the cradle of Bibliopegy as well as of Typography in the new and unsettled land of our forefathers."

Green's next extant book is Richard Mather's "Summe of Certain Sermons upon Genes: 15.6. Wherein Not only the Doctrine of Justification by Faith is Asserted and Cleared, and sundry Arguments for Justification before Faith, discussed and Answered, But Also the nature and meanes of Faith, with the Imputation of our Sins to Christ, and of Christs Righteousness to us are briefly Explained and Confirmed, Cambridg, Samuel Green, 1652," a quarto of fifty-nine pages. An introductory page, "To the Christian Reader," is signed by John Cotton and John Wilson. This is the first extant book of Richard Mather printed in New England, with the possible exception of a catechism which has not survived. There were two Dorchester catechisms, both by the first of the Mathers, minister of the church there from 1636 until his death in 1669. His grandson says in the "Magnalia:" "He published catechisms, a lesser and

The First Edition of the Revised Version
of the "Bay Psalm Book." 1651

a larger, so well formed that a Luther himself would not have been ashamed of being a learner from them." "No copy of either" was known to Dr. Trumbull as late as 1883. The "larger" ("A Catechisme Or, The Grounds and Principles of Christian Religion, set forth by way of Question and Answer") printed in 1650 in London, is described by Mr. Eames in his "Early New England Catechisms" from the American Antiquarian Society's copy; but the "lesser" catechism has vanished. In 1665 it appears that a new edition of one of the catechisms had been printed by Green, it being then voted that "the new impression of M[r] Mathers Catechismes should be payd for, out of a Towne Rate." The sum of £4 10s. was paid for the printing of the catechism, and the books were given to each family in town. This "new impression" is not extant. The first edition may have been issued by Green about the time of the appearance of "The Summe of Certain Sermons upon Genes: 15.6." Only one copy of the latter work has been publicly sold in many years — Brinley's, which brought but $90 in 1879.

The second Supplement to the Code of 1648–1649, covering the laws of 1651, 1652, and 1653, was printed by Green in 1654, in accordance with the order of the General Court of May 3 of that year; but cannot be traced at the present time. Whitmore believed this to have been a folio of some nineteen pages. During the summer of 1654 Green issued John Eliot's catechism in the Massachusetts Indian language, the earliest printed Indian book of which any record has been preserved. In September of the preceding year the Commissioners of the United Colonies wrote to Winslow: "Mr Eliot is preparing to print a Cattichisme of the Indian langwige which wee shall further (as wee may) by disbursing the charge of paper and printing out of the stock but by some due allowance shall Indeavor to Incurrage Thomas Stanton to assist in the worke; whoe is the most able Interpretor wee haue in the countrey for that Langwige that the worke may bee the more pfectly carried on." They also resolved that: "It is left to the two Commissioners for the Massachusets to giue order for the printing of five hundred or a Thousand Catechismes in the Indian langwige and to allow paper and the charge of printing." On September 25, 1654, they wrote to the Corporation in England, stating "one Cattachesme is alreddy printed and Mr Person is preparing another to sute those southwest ptes where the languige differs from theires who liue about the Massacheuesetts." The latter is Abraham Pierson's "Some Helps for the Indians," printed by Green, 1658–1659, of which but a single copy is known. The Indian catechism of 1654 has disappeared.

The first book printed in 1655 may have been President Charles Chauncy's Commencement sermon at Harvard: "Gods Mercy, shewed to his People in giving them a faithful Minister and Schooles of Learning for the continual supplyes thereof." Chauncy, whose name is spelled "Chauncey" in the title, had then been president of the college less than one year, having succeeded Dunster, deposed for his adoption of the principles of anti-pædo-baptism, on October 24, 1654. His sermon was published by Green, "with some additions," in an octavo of 61 pages, the title-page having the same ornamental border which was used in the "Cambridge Platform" of 1649. The Brinley copy is in the New York Public Library (Lenox collection). Green's two most important publications of 1655 are not now extant. These were the Book of Genesis and the Gospel of Matthew, Eliot's second and third Indian books. In a letter dated August 16, 1655, Eliot wrote of the Indians: "That which I now most follow, is, first the spreading of the Gospel into more remote places. . . . The second thing attended, is the Civilizing of them. . . . The third thing is the Printing of the Bible in their Language. Genesis is Printed, and we are upon Matthew, but our progresse is slow, and hands short." In another letter, dated from Roxbury, December 28, 1658, Matthew is referred to as being among "those pieces that were printed;" but it has long since vanished, together with the first book of the Bible, in Indian, and the Indian catechism. Later in 1655, "An Almanack for the Year 1656. By T. S.," was issued from the press. The only known copy of this almanac of sixteen pages, with eight lines of poetry at the foot of each page, is in the library of the American Antiquarian Society. Nathaniel Paine's list of their early New England imprints fails to identify "T. S.," whose little work, in point of date, is the first almanac after Oakes's "Astronomical Calculations" of 1650. Almanacs for 1651, 1652,

1653, 1654, and 1655, doubtless came from the Cambridge Press, but copies are unknown to present-day bibliographers. George Brinley, who formed an unapproachable collection of early New England almanacs, possessing, with few exceptions, the issues from 1646 to 1700, was unable to see them, and there is little chance of their discovery at this late date.

The extant issues of 1656 are two in number—a catechism and an almanac. The catechism is John Cotton's "Spiritual Milk," —"that incomparable Catechism," as Cotton Mather styles it, which, incorporated in the "New England Primer," came to be more popularly known in New England than any other catechism, with the one exception of "that Golden Composure," the Westminster Assembly's Shorter Catechism. The almanac is by "S. B.,"— Samuel Brackenbury, the compiler of the one for 1667, which gives his name in full. Brinley did not find a copy, but there is one at Worcester, in the possession of the American Antiquarian Society. Cotton's catechism was first printed, most probably, in London in 1646, under this title (suggested, perhaps, by William Crashaw's "Milke for Babes. Or, A North-Countrie Catechisme):" "Milk for Babes. Drawn out of the Breasts of both Testaments. Chiefly, for the spirituall nourishment of Boston Babes in either England: But may be of like use for any Children." This edition, often reprinted, is of only slightly greater rarity than the first New England issue, which is entitled: "Spiritual Milk for Boston Babes In either England. Drawn out of the Breasts of both Testaments for their souls nourishment But may be of like use to any Children. By John Cotton, B.D. late Teacher to the Church of Boston in New-England. Cambridg Printed by S G for Hezekiah Usher at Boston in New-England 1656." The first catechism of the mightiest man in early New England was the one for adults, "The Doctrine of the Church, to which is committed the Keyes of the Kingdome of Heaven," London, 1642. The "Spiritual Milk" is, of course, a catechism for children. It is a small octavo of eight leaves, the text ending upon the upper half of the recto of the last leaf. The edition must have been a large one, but only one copy is known,—George Livermore's, for which the New York Public Library (Lenox collection) paid $400 in 1894. On the back of the title-page is the signature of "Jno. Hull," master of the mint, who became a member of Cotton's church in Boston in 1648. At one time this copy was bound with eight other catechisms in one volume in the following order: Cotton's "Spiritual Milk for Boston Babes," 1656; Noyes's "Short Catechism," 1714; Fiske's "Watering of the Olive Plant," 1657; Norton's "Brief Cat-echisme," 1660; Seaborn Cotton's "Brief Summe of our Christian Faith," 1663; Stone's "Short Cat-echism," 1684; Fitch's "First Principles of the Doctrine of Christ," 1679; Perkins's "Foundation of Christian Religion," 1682; and the Westminster Assembly's "Shorter Catechism," 1740. Four of these are Cambridge imprints—the "Spiritual Milk," the "Olive Plant," the "Brief Catechisme," and the

"Brief Summe," and each exists in a unique copy.
Another edition of "Spiritual Milk" is supposed to
have been printed at Cambridge in 1668, but no copy
exists.

Four publications are to be recorded under the year
1657. The earliest of these was the following broadside mourning elegy: "A Copy of Verses Made by
that Reverend Man of God Mr. John Wilson, Pastor
to the first church in Boston; On the sudden Death
of Mr Joseph Brisco, Who was translated from Earth
to Heaven Jan. 1. 1657." This elegy on Brisco, who
was "translated,"

> Not by a Fiery Chariot as Elisha was,
> But by the Water, which was the outward cause.

contains thirty-four lines, headed by an introductory
quatrain. Dr. Green, who reproduced it in 1902 from
his own copy, apparently unique, believes it to have
been printed by Green soon after Brisco's death.
The paper upon which the verses were struck off is
nearly identical with that used for the Harvard
Theses of 1643 and 1647, sensibly differing from the
kind in use at a later period. To the early part of
1657 also belongs the first Chelmsford catechism—
"The Watering of the Olive Plant in Christs Garden.
Or A Short Catechism For the first Entrance of our
Chelmesford Children: Enlarged by a three-fold
Appendix By John Fisk Pastour of the Church of
Christ at Chelmesford in New-England. . . Printed by
Samuel Green at Cambridg in New-England. 1657."
This is a small octavo of 88 pages, the catechism

Spiritual
MILK
FOR
BOSTON BABES
In either ENGLAND.

Drawn out of the
Breasts of both TEST AMENTS
for their souls *nourishment*.

But may be of like use to any
Children.

By JOHN COTTON, B. D.
late Teacher to the Church of
Boston in New-England.

CAMBRIDG
Printed by S. G. for Hezekiah Usher
at Boston in New-England
5 6

Spiritual Milk for Boston Babes. 1656

itself filling pages 5–16, the remainder being devoted
to the "three-fold Appendix." It was published at
the expense of the inhabitants of Chelmsford four
years after the settling of the town, and was compiled
by their first pastor, the Rev. John Fiske, who in
1655 had removed to the town from Wenham (then
a part of Salem village), taking with him the greater
part of his flock. The preface of two pages, "To the
Church & Congregation at Chelmsford, Grace &
Peace, through Jesus Christ," is signed: "John Fiske,
Chelmesford this 25 of 1. mo. 1657." The title of the
catechism comes from Psalm 128:3: "Thy children
shall be like olive plants round about thy table." A
single copy is known—the one in the New York
Public Library (Lenox collection), which was formerly
Livermore's, bringing $106 in his sale in 1894, a sum
estimated by Dr. Green as being probably equal to
one-half of Fiske's annual salary. Haven records the
title of a 1668 edition of the "Appendix," but no one
has seen a copy. Green's next publication of 1657
may have been the third Supplement to the Code
of 1648–1649, covering the laws of 1654, 1655, 1656,
and 1657, and printed by direction of the General
Court. Whitmore thought this lost Supplement to
have been a small folio of twenty-six pages. The
fourth publication of the year is Richard Mather's
"Farewell Exhortation to the Church and People of
Dorchester in New-England," one of the most interesting of New England books, seemingly printed for
the members of his congregation during the twenty-
first year of his pastorate, and distributed among

them "on a certain Lord's Day." His grandson notes in the "Magnalia:" "Some Years before his Death (having sent over to his old Flock in Lancashire, a like Testimony of his Concernment for them) he composed and published, A Farewell Exhortation to the Church and People of Dorchester, consisting of Seven Directions, wherin his Flock might read the Design, and Spirit of his Whole Ministry among them; on a certain Lord's Day, he did, by the Hands of his Deacons, put these little Books into the Hands of his Congregation, that so whenever he should by Death take his Farewel of them, they might still remember how they had been exhorted." This "little Book" of thirty-one pages, so remarkable for personal interest, is now of superlative rarity. Brinley could not find a good copy. Mather's "like Testimony of his Concernment," sent to his old followers in England, is undoubtedly the following: "An Heart-Melting Exhortation, together with a Cordiall Consolation. By Richard Mather and William Tompson; Presented in a Letter from New-England, to their dear Countrey-men of Lancashire," London, 1650. Increase Mather's copy was in the Brinley collection.

The years 1655–1658 were principally employed by John Eliot in the Indian translation of the Bible. A catechism, and the books of Genesis and Matthew, were printed, as we have noted, 1654–1655. During the fall of 1658 Green issued for Eliot an Indian trans-lation of a portion of the Psalms of David in metre. It is referred to in the postscript to the letter to Floyd, December 28, 1658: "They [the Indians] have none of the Scriptures printed in their own Language, save Genesis, and Matthew, and a few Psalms in Meeter." No copy has been found. In the treasurer's account presented to the Commissioners, at Hartford, in September, 1659, there was a charge of £40: "To Mr. Green for printing the Psalmes and Mr. Piersons Catichisme." In September, 1660, it was resolved that: "The Commissioners for the Massachusetts are desired and Impowered to accoumpt with Mr. Green for the forty pounds payed him for printing Mr. Pierson's Cattachisme and the Psalmes." Pierson's catechism, in the dialect of the Quiripi Indians of the "south-west" parts of New England, is the "Some Helps" which is alluded to and described in detail in the chapter on "The Indian Books." Green began the printing of it about the beginning of December, 1658, but the book was not issued until the following year. Toward the end of 1658 he probably put forth "An Almanack of the Coelestial Motions for this present Year of the Christian Æra 1659. By Zech: Brigden." The compiler was Zechariah (or Zachary) Brigden, of Stonington, Conn., a member of the Harvard graduating class of 1657. Brinley's (sold with the almanacs for 1660, 1661, 1662, 1663, and 1665, to the Library of Congress for $156) formerly belonged to the Rev. Henry Flint, of Braintree (brother-in-law of Leonard Hoar, President of Harvard), and contained occasional memoranda in his handwriting, usually disguised in Greek letters.

One book wrongly attributed to 1658 is another edition of the New England version of "The Bay

Psalm Book," as revised and improved by Dunster and Lyon in 1651. The title is the same as that of the revision. The imprint reads: "Cambridge, Printed for Hezekiah Usher, of Bostoo." The date is conjectural. The book is a duodecimo, printed in double columns, sixty lines in a full column. The type, an excellent nonpareil letter, "which does not appear in any work known to have been printed in this country at that time," confused Haven. "The printing," he observed, "is executed by a good workman, and is the best that I have seen from the Cambridge press. I conclude, therefore, it could not be printed by Green before the arrival of Marmaduke Johnson in 1660; I have no doubt it was printed under Johnson's care, and, probably, soon after the Indian Bible came from the press in 1663." The type, however, is not used in any of the books printed by Johnson between 1660 and the year of his death, 1674, and the "Cambridge" mentioned in the imprint is unquestionably Cambridge, England. Dr. Trumbull notes that Usher, who sold the psalm books of 1640, 1647, and 1651, visited England in the autumn of 1657, charged with matters of business for the Commissioners of the United Colonies, and that this edition, not improbably, was printed, or contracted for, when he was in the mother country. It is possible, as Haven suggested, that Usher ordered copies to be bound up for the New England market with some of the small English Bibles printed at the old Cambridge. Brinley's copy, sold in 1879 for $90 to C. Fiske Harris, and now in the library of Brown University, is considered unique.

We now approach the last books printed by Green alone at his first press. Five imprints are assigned to this period, which covers a space of eighteen months, 1659-1660. Two of the number are broadsides: "An Humble Proposal for the Inlargement of University of Learning in New England," and "A Declaration of the General Court of the Massachusetts Holden at Boston in New England, October 18, 1659. Concerning the Execution of two Quakers," both printed in 1659. The first is represented by the copy in the Massachusetts Archives at the State House; the second is unknown in the original form, our knowledge of it being obtained from the London reprint of the same year. These, together with the third imprint, are of minor interest. The latter is "An Almanack for the Year 1660. By S. C." The compiler was the Rev. Samuel Cheever, of Marblehead, Mass., who prepared the almanac for 1661, which also bears his initials. Brinley's copy, the only one known, is in the Library of Congress. The other two imprints, now ranked among the most valuable publications of the press, are John Norton's "tractate" against the Quakers, "The Heart of New England Rent at the Blasphemies of the Present Generation," 1659, and "The Book of the General Lawes and Libertyes," 1660, the earliest extant collection of New England laws.

In 1659 Norton was regarded as the leading minister in the colony. When Cotton died in 1652, he was thought worthy above all others to succeed him as teacher of the church in Boston, and he was installed in that high office in the month in which Quakers first came to New England. His commanding abilities naturally made him the chief instigator of the persecutions of the people whose admission into the colony was opposed with barbarous bitterness. In October, 1658, the General Court ordered that there should be a writing or declaration drawn up and forthwith printed to manifest the evil of the tenets of the Quakers and the dangers of their practices. Norton was requested to compose this declaration. The result of his labors was printed by Green in May, 1659, in sixty pages, small quarto, and distributed at the public charge toward the end of that month. In this vigorous if unpolished tract Norton strove hard to prove the mischievous tendencies of the Quakers. For writing it he received a grant of five hundred acres of land. During the following year it was reprinted in London with an appendix of "Matter coming from New-England since this Book was printed." The reprint, complete with the appendix (wanting in most copies), is scarcely less rare than the original edition, which is included in few of our great collections of Americana. Brinley's copy, which sold for $110 in 1879, is in the New York Public Library (Lenox collection). Another example is in the library of the Massachusetts Historical Society.

The law book of 1660, apparently the last book printed solely by Samuel Green before the coming of the fourth Cambridge printer, is hardly less precious than that highly prized New York book, "The Laws & Acts of the General Assembly for Their Majesties

Province of New York. . . New-York, William Bradford, 1694," of which only eight copies—four of them imperfect—are known to exist. We have seen that the Code of 1648-1649 was followed by three Supplements, 1650, 1654, and 1657. During the preparation of a new revision, the issuing of Supplements was suspended. This revision was put through the press under the care of Secretary Rawson, Capt. Thomas Clark, and Major General Daniel Denison, who, as Whitmore has shown, were chiefly concerned in collecting, condensing, and arranging the new Code. It was printed by Green in an attractive folio of one hundred pages (title, one leaf; address, one leaf; Laws, pages 1-88; Table, eight pages), with this title: "The Book of the General Lawes and Libertyes concerning the inhabitants of the Massachusets, collected out of the Records of the General Court, for the several years wherin they were made and established. and now revised by the same Court, and disposed into an alphabetical order, and published by the same Authority in the General Court holden at Boston, in May, 1649. Cambridge, Printed according to Order of the General Court, 1660." The preface begins: "The Books of Lawes of the first impression, not being to be had for the supply of the Country, put us upon thoughts of a second which is an eloquent testimony respecting the rarity of the earlier Code." In his "History" Thomas said: "Only one perfect copy can now [1810] be found." Perfect copies are now in the following libraries: American Antiquarian Society (Edward Rawson's copy, with many additional

laws); Boston Athenaeum; New York Public Library
(Lenox collection); Pennsylvania Historical Society;
and State House, Mass. Brinley could not procure a
copy, which is conclusive evidence of its rarity. The
only copy offered at auction for a long period brought
£109 in London, in December, 1893, passing immediately into the New York Public Library (Lenox
collection). This is one of the finest of the perfect
copies of the book, being immaculate throughout
and practically uncut.

VI

THE INDIAN BOOKS

1654–1691

ELIOT began the study of the Massachusetts Indian language about the year 1643. His missionary labors began about three years later, Danforth's almanac for 1649 recording under the date of October, 1646, that: "Mr. Eliot began to preach to ye Indians in their owne language." In July, 1649, he wrote to Winslow: "I do very much desire to translate some parts of the Scriptures into their language, and to print some Primer wherein to initiate and teach them to read." This primer or catechism, prepared in 1651 and first used among the Indians in manuscript form, was ordered to be printed (as we have seen) in September, 1653, in an edition of "fiue hundred or a Thousand" copies. It was in print before September 25th of the next year, but has not survived. Similar is the fate of the second edition, issued in 1662, although 1,500 copies were printed. September 12, 1661, the Commissioners wrote to Hutchinson and Ashurst in England: "By the account you will find wee haue remaining 414 lb: 4: 4 stocke a great part wherof wilbee expended in printing the bible and a new Impression of a Catichisme." The following day they wrote to Hezekiah Usher in Boston: "Alsoe wee pray you take order for the printing of Mr. Elliotts Catichismes which wee vnderstand are much wanting amongst the Indians." Usher's account, presented to the Commissioners in September, 1662, contains the charge: "To printing 1500 Cattachismes, 15 l." Of the edition of 1669, a 32mo of 64 unnumbered leaves, printed by Marmaduke Johnson, the fourth Cambridge printer, the only known copy is in the library of the University of Glasgow, having been "Gifted to the Library by Mr. Jo. Kirton, Aprile 19, 1675." It contains a large and a short catechism and bears this title: "The Indian Primer; or, The way of training up of our Indian Youth in the good knowledge of God, in the knowledge of the Scriptures and in an ability to Reade. Composed by J. E. . . . Cambridge, Printed 1669." The text is in Indian, the only English portions of the book being the title, "The Lords Prayer," "The Ancient Creed," the introductory heading to the "Degrees of Christian Duties for several estates, collected out of the holy Scripture," the running head-lines, "The Numeral Letters and Figures, which serve for the ready finding of any Chapter, Psalm and Verse in the Bible or elsewhere," and "The Names and Order of the Books of the Old and New Testament." August 29, 1686, Eliot wrote to Boyle: "My humble request to your honour is, that we may again reimpose the primer and catechism; for though the last impression [1669?] be not quite spent, yet quickly they will; and I am old, ready to be gone, and desire to leave as many books as I can."

Little is known of this edition, which Samuel Green may have printed about 1687. Thomas Prince's imperfect copy, believed by Mr. Eames to be of the 1687 edition, is in the library of the Massachusetts Historical Society. This is only a fragment, lacking the title and other leaves, but seems to have been originally complete in forty leaves, signatures A, B, C, D, and E, in eights. The contents closely agree with the edition of 1669. The blank portion of one leaf once bore this inscription, in Prince's autograph: "Mr. B. Green says, composed by Mr. Eliot, & Printd at Camb. abt 1684," but only the latter part of this statement is now visible.

From the first, it was Eliot's ambition to see the whole Bible translated into the native tongue, although, as he wrote in 1651, he did not expect to see it entirely translated, "much lesse Printed," during his time. In a letter written to Thomas Thorowgood, in June, 1653, he said: "I have had a great longing desire that our Indian Language might be sanctified by the Translation of the holy Scriptures into it. . . . but I fear it will not be obtained in my dayes. I cannot stick to the work, because of my necessary attendance to my ministrie in Roxbury, and among the Indians, at sundry places, and the multiplied work, which in that kind ariseth upon me, and yet through the blessing of the Lord, I have this Winter translated the whole book of the Psalms. . . . While I live, if God please to assist me, I resolve to follow the work of translating the Scriptures." In August, 1655, his translation of Genesis was printed and Matthew was passing through the press. The entire translation was completed in the autumn or winter of 1658, and about this time "a few Psalmes in Meeter" were issued, but, together with the other precious portions of the first American Bible, have disappeared.

Toward the end of 1658 Green began to print the third Indian catechism, "Some Helps for the Indians Shewing them How to improve their natural Reason, To know the True God, and the true Christian Religion," by the Rev. Abraham Pierson, minister of Branford, in New Haven colony. This catechism, made for the use of the Quiripi Indians of south-western Connecticut, was completed by the 19th of September, 1657, and the manuscript was sent to the Corporation in England to be printed in an edition of "1500 Coppies." This manuscript was lost at sea in November, 1657, and another was prepared by Pierson in 1658 and after having been "Examined, and approved by Thomas Stanton Interpreter-General to the United Colonies for the Indian Language, and by some others of the most able Interpeters amogst us," was printed by order of the Commissioners at Cambridge. September 22, 1658, the Commissioners wrote to the Corporation: "By our last of the 16th Instant wee certifyed you of our purpose to send Mr. Persons Catichisme by the first oppertunitie to bee printed in England since which time it is come to our hands but vpon further consideration in regard of the hazard of sending and difficultie of true printing it without a fitt ouerseer of the presse by one skilled in the language wee haue chosen rather to haue it printed heer and accordingly haue taken order for the same and hope it wilbee finished within three months." Only the first sheet (sixteen pages) had been printed by Green before December 28, 1658, and, although the title-page is dated 1658, the book was not issued until the fall or early winter of 1659. The first sheet was reprinted by the Corporation in the spring of 1659 in "A further Accompt of the Progresse of the Gospel amongst the Indians in New-England," the ninth of the Eliot tracts and the rarest of that contemporary series of narratives which so faithfully chronicle the progress of missionary work among the native tribes. The completed "Some Helps," in its original form, is now known to us by the unique Lenox copy, which cost Mr. Lenox £12 12s. Some copies of this edition appear to have fallen into the hands of "that mischievous adventurer," Captain John Scott, who issued it in London with a new title-page (printed "for," not "by," Samuel Green), which announces him as being the sole examiner and approver of the book. The British Museum copy is the only extant example of this curious issue, which agrees with the other save in the title-page.

The Cambridge Press was now sorely in need of new type; in order to assure the successful publication of Eliot's Indian version of the Bible, an additional printer was needed. In June, 1658, Green petitioned the General Court as follows:

"Samuel Green, Printer at Cambridge Humbly sheweth Whereas yoᵣ poare Servant hath (althovgh with many wants & difficultyes) spent some yeares in attending ye service of ye Country in that worke of Printing, The Presse & the appurtenances thereof, w^thout a speedy svpply, & especially of letters, & those principally for ye printing of English, is now almost wholy vncapeable of farther improvem^t, either for the answering of ye Countryes expectation, or for the benefitt of such as are employed therein, & ye Colledge (to whome ye presse doth pperly belong) have not ability in theyr hands to helpe, so that vnlesse some p^rsent care bee taken by the wisdome & furtherance of this Hon^rd Court, ye improvem^t thereof must of necessity cease, & yor poore servant must bee forced to change either his habitation or employm^t or both. The consideration & supply whereof is the humble request of yor poore servant, or if not, yor determination therein, y^t so hee may more clearely see his way for ye serving of the pvidence of god in some other calling."

This petition was commended to the consideration of the Commissioners, who were desired to write to the Corporation in England for "the pcureing of 20^i worth of letters for the vse of the Indian College." In a letter written in December of the same year to the treasurer of the Corporation, Eliot requested the employment of "some honest young man, who hath skill to compose, (and the more skill in other parts of the work, the better)," to be sent over to work "at the presse in Harvard Colledge, under the Colledg Printer, in impressing the Bible in the Indian language." "The whole book of God," he concluded, "is translated into their own language, it wanteth but revising, transcribing, and printing." Under the same date, Governor Endicott asked for the provision of "papers and letters and such things as may further the work, as also a Journey man Printer to be helpefull under Mr. Greene our Printer to expedite the work. . . Mr. Eliot will be ready at all times to correct the sheets as fast they are Printed, and desireth nothing for his paines."

These letters were favorably received in England, and in the autumn of 1659 a new printing press, "printing letters for the bible," and other necessary arrangements were procured in London at the expense of the Corporation for the Propagation of the Gospel among the Indians in New England, and sent over to Cambridge. According to Dr. Trumbull, the printing of the New Testament in Indian was begun in the autumn or early winter of 1659. The first thing issued in the native tongue from the press was apparently the broadside, "A Christian Covenanting Confession," printed on one side of a quarto sheet in two parallel columns, Massachusetts Indian and English. From certain peculiarities of orthography in the Indian version of this covenanting confession, Dr. Trumbull believed it to have been printed before the New Testament. "Probably it was printed before," he said, "but not long before the gathering of the first Indian church at Natick, in 1660." The only extant copy belongs to the University of Edinburgh, to which it was presented in 1699. It was reissued about 1670, with several slight changes and a few additional words and Scripture references; and of this the only copy known is in the Congregational Library, Boston. The latter lacks a small portion of the lower right-hand corner.

Marmaduke Johnson, the new printer, did not arrive in New England until the summer of 1660. In the meantime, Samuel Green, assisted by an Indian apprentice (James the printer, later called James Printer, who was employed on both editions of the Bible), had printed sheets A to L, Matthew to John. The printing was finished in the summer of 1661, and an edition of one thousand or fifteen hundred copies was speedily published. Forty copies were sent to England for presentation purposes, with English title-pages and a dedication to Charles II in addition to the Indian title. About one-fifth of the edition was bound up separately. In 1891 Mr. Eames traced sixteen copies, Dr. Wright adding five examples to the number in 1894. The highest auction price is $700, given in 1879 for the Brinley copy (now in the New York Public Library, Lenox collection). Col. Thomas Aspinwall's copy, which brought 3s. 6d. in 1820, realized $610 at the Barlow sale in 1890. The most recent sale of the New Testament was in April, 1903, when the Appleton copy brought $590, having previously fetched $310 at the Livermore sale in 1894.

In September, 1662, the Commissioners wrote to Robert Boyle: "the bible is now about halfe done; the other halfe is like to bee finished in a yeare." The printing of the Old Testament was finished before the next meeting of the Commissioners, in September, 1663; and in December of that year that

extraordinary result of persevering industry and
pious zeal, the entire Bible in Indian, was published
in an edition of one or perhaps two thousand copies.
Twenty copies in sheets, sent to the Corporation in
England for presentation purposes, were uniformly
bound in dark blue morocco. One of these was given
to Charles II April 21, 1664, but cannot be traced to-
day. Another, given to Mary Armyne, who made
large gifts of money to the society which supported
Eliot's work, is to-day the highest priced of all copies
of the book. Presented to this lady in 1664, it was
later owned by Philip Yorke, first Earl of Hardwicke
and Lord Chancellor of England from 1737 to 1756,
"the most eminent lawyer that ever sat on the wool-
sack." After the death of the Right Hon. Charles Philip
Yorke, the fourth Earl, a portion of the Hardwicke
library was removed from Wimpole House to London,
and sold by auction June 29, 1888, when this Bible,
perhaps the finest of all known copies, was purchased
for Charles H. Kalbfleisch, of Brooklyn, for £580. A
few years later it was privately sold to Marshall C.
Lefferts, of New York City, and at the private dis-
persion of Mr. Lefferts's collection, in the fall of 1901,
was secured by Mr. E. Dwight Church for about $5,000.
  The second highest auction price for the book is the
£370 given in London, in July, 1902, for another of the
presentation copies. The latter is not merely a book
of rarity and value, but a book with a history and a
provenance of distinction, ennobled and dignified by
a long line of illustrious possessors, as a distinguished
ancestry adorns a family. We know little of its early

history, but in the late '50's it was sold as a duplicate
by the Bodleian Library, of Oxford. Henry Stevens,
of Vermont, then of London, through whose hands
passed so many Cambridge books, secured it, and in
1861 sold it to James T. Bruce, of New York City, for
one hundred guineas. The Bruce library was sold
at auction in 1868, and this Bible was purchased for
$1,130 by John A. Rice, of Chicago, George Brinley,
of Hartford, being the under-bidder at $1,127.50. At
the Rice sale in 1870 the book was resold for $1,050,
and passed into the hands of William Menzies, of New
York City, who had it rebound in brown morocco by
Francis Bedford, most famous of English binders. In
1876 the Menzies library was sold in New York, and
this volume became the property of Joseph J. Cooke,
of Providence, for the reduced sum of $900. Brayton
Ives, of New York City, was the next owner, paying
$1,250 for it at the Cooke sale in 1883. Eight years later
Mr. Ives sold his magnificent book-collection, and this
highly treasured American Bible realized $1,650. The
next owner was Clarence S. Bement, of Philadelphia,
who soon sold it again privately. It then became a
notable part of Mr. Church's collection, but upon his
purchase of the Armyne-Hardwicke-Kalbfleisch-Lef-
ferts copy, passed into the hands of the purchaser of
the Lefferts library. Consigned to London for sale at
auction in 1902, it was resold, as we have noted, for
£370, and passed immediately into the possession of a
new American owner, after having been the feature of
seven great native libraries. The complete story of its
wanderings since it left the press of Samuel Green and

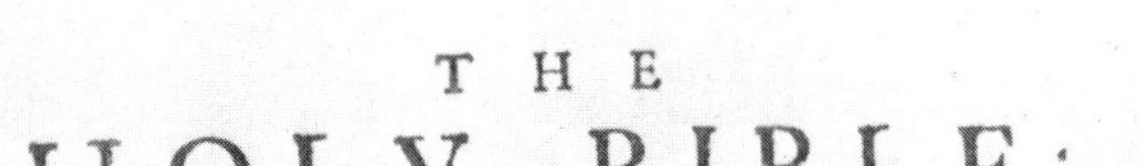

THE
HOLY BIBLE:
CONTAINING THE
OLD TESTAMENT
AND THE *NEW*.

Translated into the

INDIAN LANGUAGE,
AND

Ordered to be Printed by the *Commissioners of the United Colonies* in *NEW-ENGLAND*,

At the Charge, and with the Consent of the

CORPORATION IN ENGLAND
For the Propagation of the Gospel amongst the Indians in New-England.

CAMBRIDGE:

Printed by *Samuel Green* and *Marmaduke Johnson.*

MDCLXIII.

The Eliot Indian Bible. 1663

Marmaduke Johnson in Cambridge two hundred and forty-two years ago would read almost like a fairy tale.

The only copy known to have been in Eliot's possession is now in the library of J. Pierpont Morgan, who secured it in 1900 with the collection of the late Theodore Irwin, of Oswego, which he purchased en bloc. One leaf bears this inscription: "Thomas Shepard's book, 2, 6, 1666, ye gift of ye Revd Translator." This was the Rev. Thomas Shepard, who was born in 1635, graduated at Harvard in 1653, and was minister in Charlestown from 1659 until his death in 1677. It contains a leaf not to be found in most of the extant copies. Sir William Ashurst's copy, sold at the third Brinley sale, 1881, for $900, was acquired by Mrs. Ralph L. Cutter, of Brooklyn, a direct descendant of John Eliot. This is one of the most remarkable of the presentation or dedication copies. Thirty copies were known to Mr. Eames in 1891, when he published his "Bibliographic Notes on Eliot's Indian Bible," the standard authority upon everything connected with the Indian Apostle. To his fascinating pages we refer the readers who desire an intimate knowledge of the first Bible printed here in any tongue—that precious memorial of a forgotten nation, whose language, at the beginning of the seventeenth century, "was spoken over an area of territory half as large as Europe."

In November, 1663, Richard Baxter wrote to Eliot: "Methinks the Assemblies Catechism should be next the holy Scriptures, most worthy of your Labours." Although made and printed, this translation has not been seen in our time. Eliot's next translation in Indian was Baxter's "Call to the Unconverted," first printed in London in 1657. It was finished on the last day of 1663, sent to the press early in 1664, and published before August 25th of the same year in an edition of one thousand copies. It is now represented only by the second edition of 1688, printed by Samuel Green, five copies of which were described by Mr. Eames. In 1665 Eliot finished a translation of Lewis Bayly's "Practice of Piety," one of the most popular of the religious books of the seventeenth century, and two hundred copies were printed by Green in the same year. Three copies were known to Mr. Eames, one of which was bought for $205 for the library of Yale College at the first Brinley sale. The second edition, printed by Green, is dated 1685, but was evidently issued during the summer of 1686. August 29, 1686, Eliot wrote to Boyle: "Our Indian work yet liveth, praised be God; the bible is come forth [the second edition, finished in 1685], many hundreds bound up, and dispersed to the Indians, whose thankfulness I intimate and testify to your hononr. The Practice of Piety is also finished, and beginneth to be bound up." Six copies are known, all save one in public libraries.

Eliot's next Indian publication was "The Indian Grammar Begun: or, An Essay to bring the Indian Language into Rules. . . . Cambridge: Printed by Marmaduke Johnson. 1666," prepared with the help of his sons, John and Joseph. According to the records of the Commissioners, four hundred and fifty copies were bound in 1667; some copies may have been sent to England, "to be bound there for presents," and the entire edition could not have exceeded five hundred copies. Eight perfect examples of the book were recorded by Mr. Eames. The fine Lenox copy seems to be the one which brought £45 10s. in London, in May, 1859. The Brinley copy, which sold low in 1879 to Dr. Trumbull, is now in the Watkinson Library, Hartford. The book is a well-printed quarto of pages (4), 66. Thomas assigned it to Green's press about 1664, but could not have seen a copy, as he says "no year is mentioned" and further describes it as occasionally bound with the "Psalter," in *small octavo.* In 1672 Marmaduke Johnson printed for the use of the Indian seminary at Natick one thousand copies of Eliot's "Logick Primer. Some Logical Notions to initiate the Indians in the knowledge of the Rule of Reason; and to know how to make use thereof;" but the British Museum copy is the only extant example. This little work, a 32mo of forty unnumbered leaves, is given in the Massachusetts Indian language, with a verbatim English interlinear translation. It was issued before September 6, 1672, when the Commissioners, meeting at New Plymouth, resolved that: "Mr. Hezekiah Vsher is ordered to pay out of the Indian Stocke in his custody. . . . To Marmaduke Johnson for printing stiching and cuting of a thousand Indian Logick Primers," £6.

In 1680 a second, revised edition of the Indian New Testament, prepared with the assistance of John Cotton, of Plymouth, was put to press, but was not published until the autumn or winter of the following year, although the title-page is dated 1680. Many

copies of the first edition had been "spoyled & lost"
during the war with Philip, and the great need of
Bibles made Eliot "meditate upon a 2ᵈ impᵣssion."
Calling Cotton to his aid, Eliot "accordingly tooke
pains to revise the first edition." He obtained authority
for the printing of a new edition, but, as he wrote,
"met wᵗʰ much obstruction for reprinting the old
testamᵗ, yet by prayre to God, Patience & intreatye,
at last obteined yᵗ also." Twenty-five hundred copies
were issued of the New Testament, a few of which
may have been bound up separately for immediate use.
Two thousand copies were kept to be added to the
Old Testament, issued from the press in the fall of
1685. Of the completed Bible, published in an edition
of two thousand copies at a cost of £900, Mr. Eames
was able to trace fifty-five examples. The highest
auction price is $950, given in 1884 for the Hastings-
Brinley-Murphy copy, now in the John Carter Brown
library. The present value of a fine copy is doubtless
largely in excess of this sum.

An Indian translation of Shepard's "Sincere Convert," made about 1664, but not printed until 1689, was
the last of John Eliot's publications in the native
language, his death occurring in Roxbury, May 21, 1690,
in the eighty-sixth year of his age. It was revised for
the press by Grindal Rawson, and was printed by
Samuel Green. Mr. Eames recorded four perfect
copies. In 1691 Rawson published his own translation
of Cotton's "Spiritual Milk for Babes." This little
rarity, printed by Samuel Green and his youngest son,
Bartholomew, is the last of the Indian books issued in

Cambridge. One year later the press was inactive, printing in the first American home of typography being at an end. Mr. Eames mentioned five copies of Rawson's translation—the seventh Indian catechism. Some examples were bound with the 1689 edition of "The Sincere Convert." The New York Public Library (Lenox collection) contains a copy of each work, which were evidently bound together at one time, although they have been separated for a long period. Their former owner, an ardent contemporary admirer of the Apostle to the Indians, wrote on the verso of a blank leaf facing the title of "The Sincere Convert:" "This Mr. Eliot translated all the Bible into this N. American Language. O si sic omnia fecisset!"

VII

THE NEXT FOUR YEARS OF THE PRESS

1661-1664

WHEN Marmaduke Johnson, the new Cambridge printer, arrived in New England in the summer of 1660, the production of the Indian New Testament was well advanced, Green, aided by a native apprentice, having printed off a considerable portion—sheets A to L, Matthew to John. In addition to his labors on the New Testament, Johnson evidently assisted Green in the printing of two works, which properly belong in this chapter, although issued before 1661: John Norton's Boston catechism, made for the use of the children of his congregation, and "An Almanack for the Year 1661. By S. C. [Samuel Cheever]," the first, dated 1660, probably issued during the fall of that year, the latter issued during the last month of 1660 and post dated, both books bearing the initials of the two printers. Norton, who had been minister of the church in Ipswich from the latter part of 1638 until 1652, when he was called to the first church in Boston to succeed John Cotton, was the author of two catechisms, a larger and a lesser. The former, prepared during his ministry in Ipswich, was printed in London in 1648 with this title: "A Brief and Excellent Treatise containing the Doctrine of Godlinesse, or Living unto God.

92

Wherein the Body of Divinity is substantially proposed and methodically digested, by way of Question and Answer." No Cambridge edition of this catechism is known to have been printed. The lesser catechism, prepared for the children of his Boston flock, was printed in Cambridge three years before his death, and has a somewhat similar title: "A Brief Catechisme Containing the Doctrine of Godlines, or of living unto God." It is a small octavo of twenty-two pages. In his "Early New England Catechisms" Wilberforce Eames describes two copies (apparently the only ones known): the George Livermore example, perfect (now in the New York Public Library, Lenox collection), and the Massachusetts Historical Society copy, which lacks the title-page. According to Prince's manuscript catalogue, a second edition of the Boston catechism was printed in Cambridge in 1666, probably by the same printers; but this later edition has not been found.

During the first half of 1661 the two printers were busily engaged with the issuing of the Indian New Testament, which was published at the end of the summer of that year. An imprint assigned to 1661, on unsatisfactory evidence, and supposed to have been printed by Green alone, is a second edition of "A Short Catechism," by James Noyes,—the Newbury catechism, which, according to tradition, was printed in compliance with the recommendation of the General Court by Stephen Daye in 1641. The "first" edition is not known, nor do we know of the "second" edition. A "third" edition (Boston, 1676), mentioned in Haven's list, is also unknown to us, the earliest extant edition of this little catechism, made for the religious instruction of the children of the Newbury church, being the one printed in Boston in 1694 by Bartholomew Green, a son of Samuel Green. The almanac for 1662, printed toward the end of 1661, was by Nathaniel Chauncy, and was printed by Green alone. The Brinley copy is in the Library of Congress.

Of the four known imprints of 1662, two have disappeared: the first edition of Michael Wigglesworth's "Day of Doom," the most widely circulated poetical volume in New England during the seventeenth century, and the second edition of Eliot's short catechism for the use of the Indians, which was first printed in 1654. A third imprint of 1662 was Israel Chauncy's "Almanack for the Year 1663;" a fourth was Jonathan Mitchel's "Propositions concerning the Subject of Baptism and Consociation of Churches, Collected and Confirmed out of the Word of God, by a Synod of Elders and Messengers of the Churches Assembled at Boston In the Year 1662," the original edition of the result of the Synod of 1662, "Printed by S. G. for Hezekiah Usher at Boston in New-England." The latter work does not bear Mitchel's name, but Cotton Mather says: "Chiefly of his [Mitchel's] Composure, and when a most Elaborate Answer to that Result was published by some very worthy Persons, that were then Dissenters, the Hardest Service in the Defence was assigned to him."

Copies of the "Propositions" are in the American Antiquarian Society, Boston Public Library, John

Carter Brown, Massachusetts Historical Society collections, etc. The Rev. Jonathan Mitchel (or Mitchell; Sibley gives the former form of spelling), born in Yorkshire, England, in 1624, died in Cambridge, July 9, 1668, was styled "the darling of his time," "the matchless Mr. Mitchel," etc. He was one of the seven graduates at Harvard in 1647, his name figuring in the Theses for that year, an imperfect copy of which is preserved in the library of the Massachusetts Historical Society. On October 8, 1662, the General Court appointed Mitchel and Captain Daniel Gookin licensers of the Cambridge Press, recommending that "Mr. Mitchell doe take the oversight of the same at the presse, for the preventing of any erratas."

Early New England poetry shares with early American almanacs and early New England Primers the distinction of being extraordinarily rare. "The Day of Doom," a versification of the Scriptural account of the Last Judgment, is a striking illustration of this fact, the earliest issues being lost to us, although four editions are thought to have been printed in Cambridge 1662–1683. Its author (born in England in 1631, died in Massachusetts in 1705) was one of the numerous New England divines of English birth who wrote verses which are merely rare curiosities to-day. Yet, with the exceptions of the Bible, the Shorter Catechism, and the New England Primer, "The Day of Doom" was the most popular book of the colonial days. Cotton Mather thought it would be read until the "Day of Doom" itself would arrive, but, although eighteen hundred copies were issued of the first edition (the second, third, and fourth editions, perhaps, being equally large), no edition has come down to us with an early date. The very popularity of the book wore it out, indeed, for this gloomy "Poetical Description of the Great and Last Judgment—" this "blazing and sulphurous poem," as Prof. Tyler called it—was to be found in every Puritan home. As Sibley, in his "Harvard Graduates," observed: "This work represented the theology of the day, and, for a century, with the exception, perhaps, of the Bible, was more popular throughout New England than any other that can be named. It passed through several editions in book-form, besides being printed on broadsides and hawked about the country. As late as the early part of the last century [the Nineteenth] many persons could repeat the whole or large portions of it."

Wigglesworth, who graduated at Harvard in 1651, was the earliest poet among the graduates of the little Cambridge college. There were earlier graduates, as Dr. Green notes, who indulged at times in versification, but their attempts were confined to elegies, and short poems on minor occasions, and were not considered of literary importance. A "feeble shadow of a man," who sorrowed and ailed all his life, Wigglesworth's protracted physical infirmities and sufferings deepened his convictions of the truth of the theological doctrines of the Puritans, and he was inspired to express them in verse. According to Cotton Mather, his "Sickly Constitution so prevailed upon him as to confine him, from his Publick Work, for some whole Sevens of years. His Faithfulness continued, when his Ministry was thus interrupted. The Kindness of his Tender Flock unto him, was answered in his Kind concern to have them Served by other Hands. . . . And that he might yet more Faithfully set himself to do Good, when he could not Preach, he Wrote several Composures, wherein he proposed the Edification of such Readers, as are for Truths dressed up in a Plain Meeter."

These "Composures," written, indeed, in a painfully "Plain Meeter," were three in number: "The Day of Doom," first published in 1662; "God's Controversy with New England," describing "New England planted, prospered, declining, threatened, punished" (written "in the tine of the Great Drought" [1662] but not printed until 1871); and "Meat out of the Eater," first issued in 1670. "The Day of Doom," the most pretentious and best known of this poetical trio, was first printed, without doubt, by Green and Johnson in Cambridge in 1662. No copy of this first edition seems to be known, although, on Wigglesworth's own statement as authority, eighteen hundred copies came from the press ("of 1800 there were scarce any unsold, or but few, at ye yeer's end"). In the library of the New England Historic Genealogical Society is a fragment of "The Day of Doom," which John Ward Dean (who devoted much attention to Wigglesworth), Dr. Samuel A. Green, and other bibliographical experts believed once belonged to a copy of the first edition, 1662. The font of type used and certain ornamental initial letters and border pieces led Dr. Green to believe that this fragment belongs to an edition "probably printed by Samuel Green at Cambridge." It does not contain marginal notes or Scriptural allusions, resembling, in this respect, the London editions of 1666 and 1673, which were doubtless reprinted from the first Cambridge edition.

The second edition of "The Day of Doom" was unquestionably printed in Cambridge by Samuel Green in 1666. This edition seems to have contained the marginal notes, which were evidently used in the third Cambridge edition (circa 1673), in the fourth Cambridge edition (circa 1683), in the fifth American edition (Boston, 1701), and in later issues of the poem. The use of the notes in the second Cambridge edition is referred to as follows in a statement by the author, found in one of his manuscript note-books (now in the possession of the New England Historic Genealogical Society): "About 4 Yeers after [1666] they ['The Day of Doom'] were reprinted wth my consent, & I gave them the proofs & Margin. notes to affix." The Massachusetts Historical Society has a defective copy of "The Day of Doom," lacking the title-page and the three following leaves, which belongs, perhaps, to the second edition, as it contains a number of the Scriptural references in the margins. These marginal notes "are fewer, for the most part, than they are in the fifth and later editions which contain the same references though slightly amplified," and there is little doubt that this copy is a part of the lost second edition of 1666. Dr. Green, who makes no definite statement as to this, declares that "this copy of the poem is certainly a specimen of very early printing," and points out that similar border pieces were used by Samuel Green, the printer of the poem, in the law book of 1660, the Indian New Testament of 1661, the complete Indian Bible of 1663, Cotton's "Discourse about Civil Government in a New Plantation," 1663, and Norton's "Three Choice and Profitable Sermons," 1664, to mention only a few imprints of the same period.

The earliest known edition of "The Day of Doom" is the Boston edition of 1701, printed by Bartholomew Green and John Allen for Benjamin Eliot, which is called by the publisher "The Fifth Edition, enlarged with Scripture and Marginal Notes." Dr. Green says that the "Fifth Edition" might mean the fifth generally, or the fifth American edition; but there seems no reason to believe that Eliot included in his calculation the London reprints of 1666 and 1673, which were surreptitiously printed, without doubt, from the first Cambridge edition. We have, then, six editions of the poem issued before the eighteenth century: (1) Cambridge, 1662; (2) Cambridge, 1666; (3) London, 1666 (doubtless a reprint of the edition of 1662); (4) Cambridge, 1673; (5) London, 1673 (a reprint of the first edition); and (6) Cambridge, 1683. No perfect copies of the four Cambridge editions are known—the editions of 1662 and of 1666 are represented, perhaps, by fragments. The London edition of 1666 seems to exist in the unique copy in the British Museum; the London edition of 1673 is less rare, as there are copies in the British Museum, in the New York Public Library (Lenox collection), in the

Boston Public Library (Prince collection), and in a private library in Boston. The Boston edition of 1701, the earliest American edition represented by a complete copy, possesses considerable rarity, but several copies can be traced and others doubtless exist.

The rarest imprint of 1663, a year distinguished by the appearance of the complete Indian Bible, is the Hampton catechism, "A Brief Summe of the cheif articles of our Christian Faith, Composed in way of Question and Answer, Now Published, especially for the Benefit of the Town of Hampton. Cambridg, Printed by Samuel Green, 1663," which is represented to-day by the unique copy in the New York Public Library (Lenox collection). It was made by Seaborn Cotton, John Cotton's eldest son by his second wife, who was born at sea Aug. 12, 1633, in "The Griffin," while his parents were voyaging to New England; and was named "Seaborne" from the circumstance of his birth. He was a graduate of Harvard in 1651, and in 1657 began to preach at Hampton (then in Massachusetts, now in New Hampshire), where he died in 1686. Even in Cotton Mather's days his catechism was so rare that the greatest of Seventeenth Century New Englanders stated merely that Seaborn Cotton was the author of a catechism, adding: "We know nothing of the character of this work, nor whether any copies are still extant." Sabin's "Dictionary of Books Relating to America" copies the title from Prince's manuscript catalogue of his "New England Library;" but its compiler had seen "no other notice of the pamphlet, which has probably perished."

Even Sibley was unaware that a copy was in existence, and could give only Prince's transcript of the original title-page in his "Harvard Graduates." The George Livermore copy, acknowledged to be unique, was extant, however, in Sibley's time, and was a part of that remarkable collection of early New England catechisms, gathered by a contemporary of the Rev. Thomas Prince, which has been previously referred to. The New York Public Library (Lenox collection) acquired it at the Livermore sale in 1894.

John Higginson's "Cause of God and his People in New-England, as it was Stated and Discussed in a Sermon Preached before the Honourable General Court of the Massachusetts Colony, on the 27 day of May 1663, Being the Day of Election at Boston," printed by Green in the summer of 1663 and familiarly known as "the first Massachusetts election sermon which was printed," has long been prized as the earliest published example of that lengthy series of annual addresses. Richard Mather's election sermon of 1644, which was ordered to be printed by the General Court, but apparently never came from the press, would have robbed Higginson's discourse of its unique distinction had it been printed. This, apparently, was not done, and "The Cause of God and his People in New-England" is therefore, as Cotton Mather said, "The First Born by way of the Press, of all the Election Sermons that we have in our Libraries."

Three other religious discourses figure among the imprints of 1663: Thomas Shepard's "Church-Mem-

bership of Children and their Right to Baptisme,"
printed by Green alone: "A Discourse about Civil
Government in a New Plantation whose Design is
Religion," and "Another Essay for Investigation of
the Truth, in Answer to Two Questions, Concerning
I. The Subject of Baptism. II. The Consociation of
Churches," the two latter by John Davenport and
printed by Green and Johnson. The title-page of
Davenport's "Discourse about Civil Government"
wrongly contains the name of John Cotton, placed
there, by mistake, for that of the real author. "Another Essay for Investigation of the Truth" contains
an "Apologetical Preface to the Reader" of sixteen
pages, by Increase Mather, in which reference is
made to "the first Essay of this Reverend Author, in
manuscript." This "first Essay" was never printed.
Hence the title: "Another Essay," etc. The year's
imprints include "Severall Laws and Orders Made at
the Severall General Courts in the Years 1661, 1662,
1663," printed by Green, which was issued as a
supplement to the "Book of General Laws" of 1660.
The almanac for 1664, printed by Green and Johnson
toward the end of 1663, was compiled by Israel
Chauncy.

One of the leading controversies of this period had
special reference to the proper subjects of baptism.
The decision of the Synod of 1662 was in favor of
the doctrine that persons who had been baptized in
infancy, and whose lives were not immoral, might
claim the ordinance in behalf of their children. This
was strongly opposed by several ministers, one of

whom was President Charles Chauncy, of Harvard College, who prepared a work entitled "Anti-Synodalia Scripta Americana, or a Proposal of the Judgment of the Dissenting Messengers," which was printed in London in 1662, attached to a reprint of Mitchel's "Propositions concerning the Subject of Baptism and Consociation of Churches." To this work John Allin, of Dedham, replied in "Animadversions upon the Antisynodalia Americana, a Treatise Printed in Old England, in the Name of the Dissenting Brethren in the Synod held at Boston, 1662," a volume of extreme rarity, printed by Green and Johnson in Cambridge in 1664 for Hezekiah Usher, the Boston bookseller. Another contribution to the literature of the subject, also printed by the two printers in 1664, was the controversial "Defence of the Answer and Arguments of the Synod met at Boston in the year 1662, against the Reply made thereto by the Reverend John Davenport. . . Together with An Answer to the Apologetical Preface set before that Essay." Of this work, the first forty-six pages, designated "An Answer" on the title-page, were by Jonathan Mitchel; the "Defence," filling one hundred and two pages, was by Richard Mather. The Brinley copy, now in the New York Public Library (Lenox collection), was presented by Mather to Thomas Shepard.

With the exceptions of a second supplement to the law book of 1660, a broadside called "Conditions for New Planters in the Territories of the Duke of York," and Alex. Nowell's "Almanack for the Year 1665," all printed by Green, the other imprints of the year were religious in character. Two of these were posthumous works: "The Sincere Convert, discouvering the paucity of True Believers and the great difficulty of Saving Conversion," by Thomas Shepard, the elder; and "Three Choice and Profitable Sermons Upon Severall Texts of Scripture," by John Norton. "The Sincere Convert," later printed in Cambridge in an Indian version, by Eliot, was first printed in London in 1641, and ran through many English and American editions. The Cambridge edition, the first edition issued here, is rare. Norton's book contains, at the end, with continuous signatures but with independent paging and separate title-page, "A Copy of the Letter Returned by the Ministers of New-England to Mr. John Dury about his Pacification." Both works were printed by Green and Johnson. Another example from their press, and a work of equal rarity, is "A Discourse of the Last Judgment: or, Short Notes upon Matt. xxv. from Ver. 31. to the end of the chapter," by Samuel Whiting, pastor of the church in Lynn. According to Dr. Trumbull (Brinley catalogue, Part I), this work had not been found by him in any library catalogue which he had consulted. Several copies are now known.

VIII

THE FOURTH CAMBRIDGE PRINTER

1665–1674

As we have seen, Marmaduke Johnson, the fourth Cambridge printer, came from England in the summer of 1660, under the auspices of the Corporation for the Propagation of the Gospel among the Indians, to assist in the printing of John Eliot's Indian Bible. Writing in October, 1658, Eliot had requested Richard Floyd, the treasurer of the Corporation, to "hire some honest young man, who hath skill to compose (and the more skill in other parts of the work, the better), send him over as your servant, pay him there to his content, or ingage payment, let him serve you here in New-England at the presse in Harvard Colledge, and work under the Colledg Printer, in impressing the Bible in the Indian language."

Nothing is known of Johnson's early history. He had been bred a printer, however, and from the workmanship in the books printed by him in Cambridge one can see that he had been well trained. His title-pages, neatly set out, are attractive in appearance and superior to those of the two Dayes or Samuel Green, and his presswork, for the most part, is good. When he arrived in Cambridge, a portion (Matthew to John) of

the Indian Bible, upon which he had been engaged to
work, had been printed off by Green, aided by an Indian
apprentice. With his assistance, the printing rapidly
proceeded, and in September, 1661, the Commissioners
wrote to Richard Hutchinson and William Ashurst
in England: "The New Testament is alreddy finished
and of all the old the fiue bookes of Moses." A year
later the Commissioners wrote to Boyle: "The bible
is now about halfe done; and constant progresse
therin is made; the other halfe is like to bee finished
in a yeare."

Johnson's behavior about this time had seriously
delayed the printing of the Bible, and "constant
progresse" had not been made. The Commissioners,
writing in September, 1662, to Boyle, referred as
follows to his misconduct: "It pleased the honored
Corporation to send ouer one Marmaduke Johnson,
a printer, to attend the worke on Condition as they
will enforme you; whoe hath Caryed heer very
vnworthly of which hee hath bine openly Convicted
and sencured in some of our Courts although as yett
noe execution of sentence; peculiare fauor haueing
bine showed him with respect to the Corporation
that sent him ouer; but notwithstanding all patience
and lenitie vsed towards him hee hath proued uery
idle and naught and absented himselfe from the worke
more than halfe a yeare att one time; for want of
whose assistance the printer by his agreement with
vs was to haue the allowance of 21 lb. the which is to
bee defallcated out of his sallery in England." In
reply to this letter, Boyle wrote from London April

9, 1663: "Wee hope the bible wilbee finished by the Returne of the Shipps and then and not before wee desire to Receiue some from you. . . . Conserning Marmeduke Johnson, the Printer, wee are sorry hee hath so miscarryed by which meanes the printing of the bible hath bin retarded we are resolved to default the 21 lb. you mention out of his sallary; Mr. Elliott whose letter beares date three monthes after youers writes that, Johnson is againe Returned into the worke whose brother alsoe hath bine with vs and gives vs great assurance of his brother's Reformation and following his busines dilligently for the time to come; and hee being (as Mr. Elliott writes) an able and vsefull man in the presse wee haue thought fitt further to make tryall of him for one yeare longer and the rather because vpon Mr. Elliotts motion and the goodnes of the worke; wee haue thought fitt and ordered that the Psalmes of Dauid in meter shalbee printed in the Indian language; and soe wee hope that the said Johnson performing his promise of amendement for time to come may bee vsefull in the furthering of this worke which wee soe much desire the finnishing of."

Before the next meeting of the Commissioners the printing of the Old Testament was finished, and in September, 1663, they wrote to the Corporation in England as follows: "Some time after our last letter Marmaduke Johnson Returned to the Presse and hath carried himselfe Indifferently well since soe farr as wee know but the bible being finished and little other worke presenting, wee dismissed him att the end of the tearme you had contracted with him for; but vnderstanding youer honorable Corporation hath agreed with him for another yeare; wee shall Indeavour to Imploy him as wee can by printing the psalmes and another little Treatise of Mr. Baxters which Mr. Elliott is translateing into the Indian language which is thought may bee vsefull and profitable to the Indians." The "psalmes" referred to was an Indian metrical version, based on the English metrical version of "The Bay Psalm Book" of 1640. After this had been finished at the press, probably in November or December, 1663, it was appended to the Bible, and the book was sent to the binder. The "little Treatise of Mr. Baxters" is Richard Baxter's "Call to the Unconverted," first printed in London in 1657, which Eliot had translated into the Massachusetts Indian language. The records of the Commissioners show that it was printed in 1664 by Marmaduke Johnson, "with our owne printer," Samuel Green, and that one thousand copies were issued. No copy is now known to be extant, our knowledge of the work being obtained from the second edition in Indian, reprinted twenty-four years later in Cambridge by Green, several copies of which exist.

In August, 1664, Johnson's term of engagement was at an end. On August 25, 1664, Eliot wrote to the Commissioners at Hartford: "Touching the Presse, I thank God & yourselves for the good successe of the work in it. . . . . . My request, in respect to Mr. Johnson, is, that seeing the Lord hath made him instrumentall to finish the Bible, and Baxter, and is now returning for Engld, you would please to give him his due incouragmt, and such further countenance and commendation, as your wisdoms shall see meet to afford him." When the Commissioners met in September of the same year, they wrote to the Corporation: "Wee dismissed Marmeduke Johnson, the Printer, att the end of his tearme agreed for hauing Improued him as well as wee could for the yeare past by imploying him with our owne printer to print such Indian workes as could be prepared which hee was not able to doe alone with such other English Treatises which did present; for which allowance hath bine made proportionable to his laboure." The Commissioners seem to have had no intention of further employing Johnson, as they stated in the same letter: "For after time wee hope to haue all books for the Indians vse vpon ezier tearmes by our owene printer especially if it please youer honors to send ouer a fonte of Pica letters Roman and Italian which are much wanteing for printeing the practice of piety and other workes."

The first attempt to restrict the liberty of the press in Cambridge was made in 1655, but the bill passed only one branch of the legislature. A successful endeavor was made in October, 1662, when the General Court appointed two licensers, the Rev. Jonathan Mitchel and Captain Daniel Gookin, without whose "allowance" or approval nothing could be printed. At the next session of the legislature, in June, 1663, this law was repealed. An important contemporary document, still extant, is of extreme interest in relation to the repealing of the law. This document (which is reproduced in the present work from the unique original) gives the disposition of Thomas Danforth, "In behalfe of ye owners of ye presse & printers," and strongly protests against the arbitrary methods of the licensers. In 1665 the law was re-enacted, however, with an additional requirement concerning the place of printing. This restriction, which was aimed at Johnson, who had recently returned to the colony with a new printing press and "letters" (type), reads as follows:

May 27, 1665:
Ffor the prventinge of Irregularities & abuse to the Authoritie of the Country by the printinge presse
It is Ordered by this Court & authoritie thereof there shalbe no printing presses allowed in any towne within this Jurisdiction but in Cambridge nor shall any Pson or Psons prsume to print any coppie but by the allowance first had & obtayned under the hands of such as this Court shall from time to time empowre thereunto, & for the prsent doe nominate & empowre Capt. Daniel Gookin mr. Tho: Danforth prsent prsident of the Colledge & mr. Jonathan Mitchell or any three of them duely to survay such coppie or coppies as afforesd & in case of non observance of this order to forfeit the prese to the country & be disabled from using any such professiō wthin this Jurisdictiō for the time to come, provided this order shall not extend to the obstruction of any Coppie which this Court shall judge meet to order to be published in print the deputs have past this desireinge the consent of or Honord magists.

1663

Whereas at ye last Session of this Courte: Capt. Daniel. Gookin &
m^r Mitchell were nominated & impowred for ye allowing of such
Coppies as were p^r sented to ye printing p^r esse at Cambridge.
who refusing to allow of any Coppies. or to accept ye trust
comitted to y^m. The interruption thereby is greatly to y^e
Damage of the printer, & owner of the presse. who do
joyntly desire the favor of this Court, that some other meet persons y^t
are willing to accept such a trust. may be impowred or y^t otherwise ye intanglem^t
hereby put vpon the printer & owner of ye presse may be released

The Court sees meete to sett the   Thomas Danforth. In behalfe of y^e
presse at the liberty as formerly till   owner of ye presse & printer.
this Court shall take further heed
ye late ord^r is hereby repealed, their
brethren the deputs Consenting hereto:
2^d June: 1663   Edw: Rawson Secret

          The deputs Consent hereto
          William Torrey Cleric

Johnson's intention to set up his press in Boston was successfully frustrated by this act, which was passed especially to prevent him. In a petition to the General Court, in February, 1668, he declared that "Yo^r petitioner by the good hand & providence of God returning from England in the year 1665 with his printing press, & letters, and finding no law of the Country, nor order of any Court to prohibit ye Exercise of his calling in any town, or place convenient within this Jurisdiction, did apply himself (according to the Custome of strangers) to the Selectmen of the Town of Boston, for their admittance of him into that town to inhabit: In which juncture of time, yor petit^{or}ioner was informed that an order had passed this Hon^ored Court, prohibiting the Exercise of printing in any town within this Jurisdiction, save only at Cambridge." "Whereupon," Johnson continued, "yor petitioner did yield ready obedience thereunto, and tooke Cambridge for his place of abode."

During the period extending from the spring of 1665 to the fall of 1674 Johnson printed in Cambridge at his new press thirty-nine books and pamphlets, both singly and in conjunction with Green. Haven's list of early American imprints (in the second edition of Thomas's "History of Printing in America") gives the titles of ten works issued by Johnson alone during this decade: the bibliographical list at the end of this volume gives the titles of twenty works printed by him during this period. Nineteen works were issued in connection with Green. There was doubtless no regular partnership between the two printers, however, but, as Dr. Green has suggested, their presses were presumably set up in the same building, and perhaps in the same room, which partly accounts for their close business relations. At this time Green's press was worked in the Indian College, which was used "to accommodate English scholars, and for placing and using a printing press belonging to the College."

The first book printed independently by Johnson at his new press is one of the rarest works in the long list of the rare publications of the Indian Apostle—John Eliot's "Communion of Churches: or, The Divine Management of Gospel Churches by the Ordinance of Councils, Constituted in Order according to the Scriptures. . . . . . . Written by John Eliot, Teacher of Roxbury in N. E.," which, printed in 1665, has long had the distinction of being "the first privately printed American book." The verso of the title-page reads: "Although a few Copies of this small Script are Printed; yet it is not published, onely committed privately to some Godly and Able hands, to be Viewed, Corrected, Amended, or Rejected, as it shall be found to hold weight in the Sanctuary Ballance or not. . . . The procuring of half so many copies written and corrected, would be more difficult and chargeable, then the Printing of these few." The object of the tract was to "defend the utility of councils or synods, and to inculcate respect for their decisions, as the safeguards of order, discipline, and purity of faith in the churches." The Menzies copy, uncut, and with manuscript alterations by a contemporary hand (perhaps by Eliot), sold for $155 in 1876, and was believed by Joseph Sabin to be unique. The Brinley copy, uncut, which is now in the New York Public Library (Lenox collection), having brought the extremely low price of $110, was also once thought to be the only extant copy. The book is now known, however, to exist in more than these two copies. No other work was issued here in this private manner until 1692, when John Allen printed in Boston Cotton Mather's "A Midnight Cry. An Essay for our Awakening out of a Sinful Sleep," the preface of which states: "I have ordered a Small Impression. . . So that perhaps I may say of this Book, as the Philosopher did of his, 'Tis Published, but Scarce made Publick."

Eliot's friendly feeling toward Johnson, already shown by the extract quoted from his letter to the Commissioners of August, 1664, was further proved by the passing of no less than five of his publications through the Englishman's press: the "Communion of Churches," 1665; "The Indian Grammar Begun," 1666; "The Indian Primer," 1669; "Indian Dialogues," 1671; and "The Logick Primer," 1672. The title, in full, of the second work in this list is: "The Indian Grammar Begun: or, An Essay to bring the Indian Language into Rules, For the Help of such as desire to Learn the same, for the furtherance of the Gospel among them." The language of which this grammar treats was specifically that of the Massachusetts tribes of Indians, dwelling near the sea coast of the present

State of Massachusetts. According to Dr. Trumbull,
"it was spoken, with some differences of dialect which
cannot now be accurately indicated, by the Wam-
panoags of Plymouth colony, the Narragansets and
Niantics, the islanders of Nope (Martha's Vineyard),
the Montauks, &c." Dr. Trumbull thought that five
hundred copies were printed. The records of the
Commissioners contain a charge for the binding of
four hundred and fifty copies. Mr. Eames thinks that
some copies may have been sent to England in sheets,
to be bound there for presents. Nine copies are now
known, all save one in public libraries.

Johnson's other publications of 1666, two in number, have disappeared: the second edition of Norton's
"Brief Catechism," which, according to Prince's manuscript catalogue, was issued in 1666, and the second
edition of Wigglesworth's "Day of Doom," which was
undoubtedly printed this year. Johnson aided Green
in the printing of these second editions. No book is
known to have been printed by Johnson in 1667—a
barren year, during which Green's press, prolific about
this period, printed only two works, a broadside and an
almanac. The next year, 1668, was a busy one with
Johnson, as he printed, with the senior Cambridge
printer, an almanac, and, at his own press, eight works,
including a broadside. The almanac was Joseph
Browne's " Almanack for the Year 1669." The broadside, entitled "To the Elders and Ministers of every
Town within the Jurisdiction of the Massachusets in
New-England," bears no printer's name, but was evidently from Johnson's press. A copy is preserved in

the library of the Massachusetts Historical Society. Of the seven other works issued by Johnson in 1668, two books are now extant, although long thought to be lost; one book can perhaps be identified with a volume printed by Johnson and Green two years later; the remaining four imprints are not in existence.

The General Court had ordered in 1667 that no books should be printed without license, under penalty of a fine of five pounds and forfeiture of all the copies printed. On September 8, 1668, Samuel Green and Marmaduke Johnson were summoned before the Council in Boston, and were ordered to give an account of what books they had lately printed, and by what authority they were issued. The list submitted by Johnson contained six titles, all of which were probably issued in 1668:

[1] "he printed the primer: &
[2] ye psalter:
[3] Meditations on death & eternity
[4] ye Rise spring &c of ye Annabaptists
[5] Isle of Pines:
[6] ye Righteous mans euidenc for heauen
by Mr Rogrs he had licenc for all by mr.
Presidnt & mr. Chancey but ye Isle of
Pines."

The third title in this list, " Meditations on death & eternity," is probably "Daily Meditations. By Philip Pain, who lately suffering shipwrack was drowned," which was printed by Johnson, in conjunction with Green, in 1670. A copy is in the library of the Massachusetts Historical Society. The fourth title, "ye Rise spring &c of ye Annabaptists," can be identified with "The Rise, Spring, and Foundation of the Anabaptists, or Re-Baptized of our Time. Written in French by Guy de Brez, 1565 . . . . and Translated for the use of his Countrymen by J. S.," of which two copies are known, those in the libraries of the American Antiquarian Society and the Massachusetts Historical Society. The translator, Joshua Scottow ("J. S."), published in Boston in 1694 the historical "Narrative of the Planting of the Massachusets Colony Anno 1628." The colophon of "The Rise, Spring, and Foundation of the Anabaptists" says: "Printed and are to be sold by Marmaduke Johnson," showing that Johnson, in this instance, at least, was bookseller as well as printer. The "Finis" in the middle of the last page of Scottow's translated work is followed by a notice of "The Righteous Man's Evidence for Heaven," by Timothy Rogers, which was "now in the Press, and will very shortly be extant." The latter work is the sixth title in the list submitted by Johnson to the Council in 1668. No copy is known.

The first title in Johnson's list, "the primer," may possibly have been the long searched for first edition of the New England Primer, "the little Bible of New England," which for nearly two centuries was used both as a text-book for primary training and as an elementary spiritual guide. The late Paul Leicester Ford believed that the first edition of the New England Primer was issued at a much later date, stating that it was printed by Benjamin Harris in Boston

Communion of Churches:

OR,

The Divine Management of *Gospel-Churches*
by the Ordinance of

COUNCILS,

Constituted in Order according to the
SCRIPTURES.

AS ALSO,

The Way of bringing all Christian
Parishes to be particular Reforming
Congregationall Churches :

Humbly Proposed,

As a Way which hath so much Light from the
Scriptures of Truth, as that it may lawfully be
Submitted unto by all ; and may, by the blessing
of the Lord, be a Means of Uniting those two
Holy and Eminent PARTIES,

The *Presbyterians* and the *Congregationals.*

AS ALSO

To Prepare for the hoped-for Resurrection of the
Churches ; and to Propose a way to bring all
Christian Nations unto an Unity of the
Faith and Order of the Gospel.

Written by *John Eliot,* Teacher of
Roxbury in *N. E.*

Psal. 1. 10 *That ye may try the things that are excellent.*
1 John 4 1. *Try the Spirits.*

Cambridge : Printed by *Marmaduke Johnson.* 1665.

Communion of Churches. 1665

"between 1687 and 1690." The earliest known edition is that of 1727, printed in Boston in that year by S. Kneeland and T. Green, the only extant example of which (in slightly defective condition) is in the New York Public Library (Lenox collection). Mr. Eames included the title of the 1668 "primer" among the "miscellaneous catechisms" in his "Early New England Primers," querying it, and adding: "If the Primer mentioned in the first title of this list [Johnson's] was not in Indian, and if it was anything like the later New England Primers in character, it is probable that it contained something of a catechism." "ye psalter," the second title in Johnson's list, may have been a reprint of the revised "Bay Psalm Book" of 1651. No copy is extant. The fifth title, "Isle of Pines," is also lost, a fact due to the probable suppression of the entire edition by the General Court. For the unauthorized printing of the book Johnson was fined five pounds, and he appealed to the Governor and the Council to remit the fine in the following words, "The humble petition of Marmaduke Johnson of Cambridge, Printer:"

That yor Petition^r doth with all humility acknowledge his rashness & inadvertency in printing a late pamphlet (called, The Isle of Pines) without due Order & license first had & obtain'd; for which being sumõned before their honorable Councill upon his Confession & conviction, was find in the sum of five pounds to the Comonwealth. Now may it please this honoured Councill, yor Petition^r having in that act no intent or design to contemn Authority, or to

vend or publish anything that might be displeasing
thereto (as may appear by his affixing his Name to
the said Pamphlett) but only in the hope of procuring
something to himself thereby for his necessary sub-
sistence; his calling in this Country being very chargeable, his living thereon difficult, the gain thereby
uncertain, & his losse by printing frequent: He
therefore humbly prayes this honoured Councill, (if
it may seem good to yor wisdomes) that the said fine
may be remitted unto him, & be discharged him from
the payment thereof.

This eloquent appeal seems to have touched the
hearts of the matter of fact authorities, for the fine
was remitted. The suppressed work, which has been
described as "a pamphlet of the Baron Munchausen
order," was evidently reprinted by Johnson soon after
its original publication in London. The first English
edition bears, in part, the following title: "The Isle
of Pines, or a Late Discovery of a Fourth Island in
Terra Incognita. Being a True Relation of certain
English Persons who in the Dayes of Queen Elizabeth
making a voyage to the East India were cast away
and wrecked on the Island near to the Coast of Terra
Australis Incognita, and all drowned except One
man and four Women. . . . . London, 1668."
Later in 1668 a continuation appeared with this title:
"A New and Further Discovery of the Isle of Pines."
The author of "The Isle of Pines" was Henry Nevile,
an English poet and miscellaneous writer (1620–1694).
Green's list of seven titles submitted to the Council
in 1668 contains the following title: "a narration of

ye plague & fier at London," which, however, was not printed by him but by Johnson, as it is evidently this work, a copy of which is in the library of the American Antiquarian Society: "God's Terrible Voice in the City of London. Wherein you have the Narration of the Two late Dreadful Judgements of Plague and Fire, Inflicted by the Lord upon that City, the former in 1665, the latter in 1666. By T. V. Cambridge: Printed by Marmaduke Johnson, 1668."

In 1669 Johnson printed one book, "The Indian Primer," and assisted Green in the production of five other works. "The Indian Primer," of which an extensive edition was printed, is in the Massachusetts Indian language. The copy in the library of the University of Edinburgh, where it has rested since 1675, is unique. The title-page does not give the printer's name, the imprint reading: "Cambridge, Printed 1669." The five books printed with Green include an almanac ("An Almanack for the Year 1670. By J. R."); Thomas Walley's "Balm in Gilead to heal Sions Wounds," the first edition; Davenport's "God's Call to His People To Turn unto Him; Together with His Promise to Turn unto Them," printed for the son of Hezekiah Usher; the Earl of Winchilsea's "True and Exact Relation of the Late Prodigious Earthquake & Eruption of Mount Etna;" and Nathaniel Morton's "New-Englands Memoriall," the first work of importance not wholly religious in character which was printed in New England. Davenport's "God's Call" was the first work to bear the name of John Usher, the son of the publisher of

"The Bay Psalm Book" and other early New England books. The latest work printed for the father was Norton's "Three Choice and Profitable Sermons," 1664, printed by Green and Johnson. "New-Englands Memoriall," compiled by its author, who was Secretary of the Colony, from Bradford's and Winslow's manuscript journals, is inexpressibly rare in fine condition. Sabin said in 1880: "Concerning the extreme rarity of the first edition of this important work, it will be sufficient to remark that we know of but three perfect copies in the United States,"—an observation which is not strictly true to-day. The book, which is a stout quarto of pages (12), 198, (10), was printed by the two Cambridge printers for John Usher, who had succeeded to his father's book business. The finest copy of this historical monument which has been publicly offered for a long period is the splendid example, in full crimson crushed levant morocco, tooled to an old English "cottage" pattern, with doublure of green crushed levant morocco, inlaid in crimson morocco, and handsomely tooled, which was once in the library of John Evelyn, the diarist and bears his autograph signature and motto, and latterly was in the possession of Marshall Clifford Lefferts, of New York City. At a London auction sale, in 1903, of a portion of Mr. Lefferts's collection of Americana, this copy sold for £87 to an English rare book dealer, who priced it at £142, a sum considerably nearer its true value.

Eight works were printed by Johnson and Green in 1670; the second edition of Walley's "Balm in Gilead,"

Pain's "Daily Meditations," Increase Mather's "Life and Death of Mr. Richard Mather," the first edition of Wigglesworth's "Meat out of the Eater," William Stoughton's "New England's True Interest not to Lie," John Oxenbridge's "Quickening Word for the hastening a Sluggish Soul to a seasonable Answer to The Divine Call," Davenport's "Sermon Preach'd at the Election of the Governor, at Boston in New-England, May 19th, 1669," and "An Almanack for the Year 1671. By D. R. [Daniel Russell]." The 1670 edition of Walley's "Balm in Gilead," long thought to be simply a re-issue of the 1669 edition, is a distinct and separate edition,—an interesting fact recently noted by Doctor Green. With few exceptions, the second edition was printed line for line from the first edition. In addition, the second edition contains the following important advertisement: "There is now going to the Press sundry excellent and divine Poems, entitled, Meat out of the Eater; or, Meditations concerning the Necessity, End, and Usefulness of Afflictions unto Gods Children; All tending to prepare them for, and comfort them under the Cross. By Michael Wigglesworth." No copy of this first edition of this famous New England book is now in existence, and probably has not been extant since the latter part of the seventeenth century. The earliest edition known to collectors is the fourth, printed in Boston in 1689 by Richard Pierce for John Usher. Wigglesworth, who noted in one of his manuscript journals that he had "been long employed in a great work composing Poems about ye Cross" ["Meat out of the Eater,"] finished his task October 28, 1669, "my Birth day & ye birth day of this Book."

Increase Mather's "Life and Death" of his father was the second of his acknowledged publications. His name does not appear on the title-page, but is signed to the dedicatory address. It has been called "the first of his works printed in New England," which is probably the case, as "The Mystery of Israel's Salvation Explained and Applyed," 1669, which transatlantic cataloguers have carelessly or wilfully attributed to a Cambridge press, was printed, without doubt, in London. Of Stoughton's Dorchester sermon, "New England's True Interest not to Lie," two editions were printed in 1670, the title-page of the second edition agreeing with that of the first edition, the remainder of the volume being set up anew. The later edition affords a curious instance of the scarcity of paper at this period, pages 39–40 containing in smaller type the matter given on pages 36–38, the printers thus saving a signature by the compression of this portion of the text. This sermon contains the frequently quoted sentence: "God sifted a whole Nation that he might send choice Grain over into the Wilderness." Davenport's "Sermon Preach'd at the Election of the Governor" bears the brief statement: "Printed in the Year 1670," which recently so confused a Philadelphia cataloguer that he described the book as a Boston imprint! The rarest imprint of 1670, with the notable exception of the lost first edition of "Meat out of the Eater," is Oxenbridge's "Quickening Word for the hastening a Sluggish Soul to a seasonable Answer to The Divine Call. Published by a poor Sinner that found it such to him. Being the last Sermon Preached in the First Church of Boston Upon Isaiah 55. 6. By the Pastor there, [John Oxenbridge] on the 24th of the fifth Month, 1670." Cotton Mather, with his customary carelessness, noted in the "Magnalia" that Oxenbridge "published a Sermon about Seasonable seeking of God," an inexact entry which has misled all modern writers on early New England religious subjects and all collectors of early New England books, even mystifying George Brinley, most successful of New England bibliophiles, who possessed a copy of the book and entered it as anonymous, not identifying it with Mather's "Sermon about Seasonable Seeking." Dr. Trumbull, in describing the Brinley copy, which sold for the extremely low price of $45, first identified the sermon as Oxenbridge's. This copy is now in the New York Public Library (Lenox collection). No other example seems to be known.

Johnson's publications in 1671 were five in number: Samuel Danforth's "Brief Recognition of New-Englands Errand into the Wilderness" (Massachusetts election sermon); Mitchel's "Nehemiah on the Wall in Troublesom Times; or, A Serious and Seasonable Improvement of that great Example of Magistratical Piety and Prudence, Self-denial and Tenderness, Fearlessness and Fidelity, unto Instruction and Encouragement of present and succeeding Rulers in our Israel" (Massachusetts election sermon, preached in 1667); Eleazer Mather's "Serious Exhortation to the Pres-

ent and Succeeding Generation in New-England. . . .
Being the Substance of the Last Sermons Preached by
Eleazer Mather, late Pastor [in Northampton];" John
Eliot's "Indian Dialogues," one of the rarest of the
Cambridge imprints; and "A Platform of Church-
Discipline Gathered out of the Word of God," the
second American edition of the "Cambridge Platform." The rarest of the first three works (all three
printed with Green) is Eleazer Mather's "Serious
Exhortation," the only published work of the first
minister of Northampton, Mass., who died in 1669.
It is prefaced by a five page "Address to the Church
and Inhabitants of Northampton," written by the author's younger brother, Increase Mather. A second
edition, of almost equal rarity, was printed in Boston
in 1678 by John Foster. The "Cambridge Platform"
of 1671 and Eliot's "Indian Dialogues" were printed
by Johnson alone. The former, of great rarity in fine
condition (copies in ordinary condition are common
enough), is one of Johnson's best printed books; the
latter, a crudely gotten up production, typographically considered, is one of the least common and most
fascinating volumes in the brief list of early Indian
Americana.
The "Indian Dialogues," entirely in English, were
intended by Eliot for the use of the native Indian
teachers and ministers, "For Their Instruction in that
great Service of Christ, in calling home their Countrymen to the Knowledge of God, And of Themselves,
and of Jesus Christ." The title-page does not give
Eliot's name. In the preface, signed "J. E.," he re-

marked: "These Dialogues are partly Historical, of some things that were done and said; and partly Instructive, to shew what might or should have been said, or that may be (by the Lords assistance) hereafter done and said, upon the like occasion. . . . For sundry weighty Reasons I desire and endeavour, that our Learned Indians should learn at least the English Tongue; our Indian Churches holding communion with the English Churches, must perform that Service in the English Tongue. If the Lord give life, and length of dayes, I may hereafter put forth these or the like Dialogues in the Indian Tongue." The little volume, a very small quarto, does not bear Johnson's name, the imprint saying: "Printed at Cambridge. 1671;" it contains title-page, one leaf; "Dedication," two leaves; and text, pages 1–81 (pages 61–66 omitted in the pagination). Two copies are known,— one in the Bodleian Library, Oxford, and one in the New York Public Library (Lenox collection). The latter, once in the Jolley collection, cost James Lenox only £5 5s. It is a fine, clean example, in the original sheep, with the original blank leaves at beginning and end. It contains three manuscript corrections in a contemporary hand, perhaps Eliot's.

"The Logick Primer," in Indian and English, which Johnson printed in 1672, his sole publication during that year, was also prepared by Eliot for the instruction of the native teachers. The full title is: "The Logick Primer. Some Logical Notions to initiate the Indians in the knowledge of the Rule of Reason; and to know how to make use thereof. Especially for the

Instruction of such as are Teachers among them. Composed by J. E. for the use of the Praying Indians. . . . Printed by M. J. 1672." This precious 32mo of forty unnumbered leaves was issued in an edition of one thousand copies, but the only known copy is the one in the British Museum.

Three books were issued by Johnson in 1673: "Old Mr. Dod's Sayings; or, A Posie gathered out of Mr. Dod's Garden. The Rev. John Dod. Collected by R. T.," a curious small octavo of only small thirteen pages; Samuel Wakeman's "A Young Man's Legacy to the Rising Generation: Being a Sermon Preached upon the Death, and at the Desire of John Tappin of Boston; Who deceased at Fairfield, the 10th of October 1672. being in the Nineteenth year of his Age;" and Increase Mather's "Wo to Drunkards. Two Sermons Testifying against the Sin of Drunkenness." The latter, which was "sold by Edmund Ranger, Bookbinder in Boston," was the third of Increase Mather's published works and the second of his publications printed in New England. Johnson used Hebrew type, in a marginal note, on page 9, and Greek type on page 3. The finest of the two Brinley copies was presented by the author to his brother, Nathanael Mather, of Dublin. Dr. Trumbull noted that "it ought, perhaps, to be described as large paper," but it is a question whether any of the Cambridge books was issued on large paper.

The publications of the fourth Cambridge printer during his last year of printing, 1674, were also three in number: Samuel Torrey's "Exhortation unto Reformation. Massachusetts Election Sermon, May 27, 1674;" "The Cry of Sodom Enquired Into. . . By S. D. [Samuel Danforth];" and Increase Mather's "The Day of Trouble is near. Two Sermons wherein is shewed What are the Signs of a Day of Trouble being near." Brinley had two copies of the last named rare work, the finer of the two bearing a presentation inscription, in the author's autograph, to Nathanael Collins of Middletown, Conn., who later inspired his son's inexpressibly rare "Elegy," printed in Boston in 1685. A vastly more interesting copy is in a Boston private library, bound in a quarto volume with fourteen other publications of Increase Mather, all the author's own copies.

Johnson's last publication of 1674, and the last book printed by him, was probably Torrey's Election sermon, issued, perhaps, in June of that year. On May 27, 1674, he petitioned the General Court to be allowed to set up his press in Boston:

The humble Petition of Marmaduke Johnson of Cambridge, Printer:

Sheweth,
That yor pet^r being in London brought up in the Art of Printing, & in no other Calling or Occupation; & being by the Providence of God brought into this Country with his Press & Letters in the year 1665. It pleased this hon^d Court (after his arrivall) to pass an Order bearing date the 3^d of May in the year aforesaid, thereby prohibiting the exercise of Printing in any Town within this Jurisdiction, save only at

Cambridge: In obedience wherevnto yor pet^r hath
ever since made that his place of residence.

But finding by long & sad Experience the great
discomodity & detriment by such Confinement of
his Calling, & an absolute impossibility of providing
comfortably for himself & family by the Incomes
thereof, though managed with greatest Care, &
followed with all possible diligence, not having im-
ployment therein for one third part of his time, Con-
flicting with difficulties too great & many to be here
recited: And also being sensible of the loss & disad-
vantage accreiving hereby to the Comonwealth, who
by his Art & Endeavo^{rs} might have many usefull &
profitable Tracts printed and published here, were he
allowed the liberty of his Calling in a convenient
place of Trade: And humbly conceiving, no more
security to the State, in preventing the printing things
irregular, or abusive therevnto, by such Confinement,
then if it were exercised in the most popul[ous]
Town within this jurisdiction; all which yor pet^r is
ready to demonstrate, if called therevnto:

Doth therefore in all humility pray this hon Court,
that you would be pleased to take the premises into
yor grave & serious Condiderations, & grant him
such liberty & relief therein as in yor wisdomes shall
seem meet; that so the Art of Printing may by this
hond: Court be duely incouraged, & the practition^{rs}
thereof have lawfull liberty of exercising the same
in sych place within this Jurisdiction, as they shall
finde most comodius for them, & most to the ad-
vantage of the Comonwealth; submitting at all times
to such Laws & Orders as are or shall be made
concerning the premises, by the Authority of this
Comonwealth.

This petition was granted May 30, 1674, and Johnson removed in August, 1674, to Boston, where he was taken sick, and died December 25 of the same year. If he had lived, he would have been the first printer in Boston, an honor which belongs to John Foster, who purchased Johnson's press and types and began printing early in 1675.

In all Marmaduke Johnson printed fifty-nine books, pamphlets, and broadsides in Cambridge: twenty publications produced in conjunction with Samuel Green, 1660–1664; twenty publications alone, at his new press, 1665–1674; and nineteen publications, in connection with Green, 1666–1671. Johnson's conduct in Cambridge did not meet with the approval of his Puritan neighbors; he got into debt, drank, and is said to have made love to Green's daughter, although he had left a wife in London. Our concern, however, is not with Marmaduke Johnson's private life, but with his career here as a printer. He was the first skilled typographer to exercise his calling in English America, and his name is connected with the best printing executed in the colonies before the eighteenth century.

IX

THE THIRD CAMBRIDGE PRINTER (1665–1674)
AND THE LAST YEARS OF THE PRESS

1675–1692

DURING 1665–1674, the period of Marmaduke Johnson's second connection with the Cambridge press, Samuel Green printed independently forty-five publications; during six years of this period, 1666–1671, he printed, in conjunction with Johnson, nineteen works, which have been described in the preceding chapter. The principal work issued by Green in 1665 was the first edition of Eliot's Indian translation of Bayly's "Practice of Piety," which has been mentioned in the account of the Indian books. Two catechisms were "printed" in 1665: Richard Mather's "Dorchester Catechism," a " new impression," and "The Assembly's Shorter Catechism, divided into 52 Parts," the title of which is given in the addenda to Haven's list. The latter, if printed, was the earliest American edition of the Westminster Assembly's Shorter Catechism, first printed in London, for official use, in 1647, and, for public use, in 1648. Both catechisms have vanished. An excessively rare imprint of this year is " A Direction for a Publick Profession in the

Church Assembly, after Private Examination by the Elders." The copy (perhaps unique) in the library of the Massachusetts Historical Society bears the following inscription, in the autograph of Governor John Winthrop, Jr.: "The Author is Mr. John Higenson, Pastor of ye Church of Salem." The most interesting imprint of 1655 is "A Funeral Elegie (Written many Years since) On the Death of the Memorable and truly Honourable John Winthrope Esq," a quarto broadside, an apparently unique copy of which is in the library of Robert C. Winthrop, Jr. It contains two columns in verse, signed "Perciful Lowle" (Percival Lowell, of Newbury, who died Jan. 8, 1665). In Dr. Green's opinion, this broadside was not printed at the time of composition but was issued soon after the author's death. The two almanacs of the year are Samuel Danforth's "Astronomical Description of the late Comet or Blazing Star, as it appeared in New-England in November, December, January, and in the beginning of February, 1664," and Josiah Flint's "Almanack for the Year 1666." Danforth's description of the comet of 1664 contains a brief theological application. He maintained that a comet was a heavenly body, moving according to defined laws, and that its appearance is portentous. The London reprint of 1666 was described as "excessively rare" in 1898 by an English book dealer, who stated that he could find no trace of the original Cambridge edition. A copy, however, is in the British Museum; another example is in the Massachusetts Historical Society library; a third copy (formerly

Barlow's) is in the New York Public Library (Lenox collection).

Green's separate imprints of 1666 included a rare work by Samuel Whiting, "Abraham's Humble Intercession for Sodom, and the Lord's gracious Concessions in Answer thereunto," and Samuel Brackenbury's "Almanack for the Year 1667." In 1667 he seems to have produced a broadside and an almanac, the latter compiled for 1668 by Joseph Dudley. In 1668, a busy year with him, he printed ten books, only two of which are extant: Thomas Shepard's "Wine for Gospel Wantons, or Cautions against Spirituall Drunkenness," and Joseph Browne's "Almanack for the Year 1669," printed with Johnson. From the addenda to Haven's list we learn that Green issued two catechisms in 1668: the second American edition of Cotton's "Spiritual Milk for Boston Babes" (first printed by Green in 1656), and an "Appendix of Catechism, Touching Church Government," by John Fiske, author of "The Watering of the Olive Plant," issued from Green's press in 1657. These catechisms are no longer extant. The other imprints of the year, six in number, are given in the list submitted by Green to the Council in September, 1668, when he was ordered to give an account of the books recently printed by him:

[1] "a Drop of Honey he printed for himself—
2   ye Rule of ye new Creature:
3   ye way to a blessed Estate in this life.
4   The Assembly of Divines Chatchise
5   a narration of ye plague & fier at London.

6   Tidings from Roome the grand Trappan
7   yt he had licenc for them all from: **ye President**
& Mr Michelle & ye young mans monitor."

The fifth title, "a narration of ye plague & fier at London," is evidently "God's Terrible Voice in the City of London. Wherein you have the Narration of the Two late Dreadful Judgements of Plague and Fire, Inflicted by the Lord upon that City, the former in 1665, the latter in 1666. By T. V.," which was not printed by Green, however, the only copy which seems to have been preserved bearing in its imprint the name of Marmaduke Johnson. The other six books are not known to-day. The first title in the list apparently refers to a lost edition (the second American) of the Westminster Assembly's Shorter Catechism.

The most interesting event of 1668 was the death, in Cambridge, on December 22, of Stephen Daye, the first printer at the first Cambridge press, among whose typographical labors was the production, in 1640, of the first edition of "The Bay Psalm Book," the earliest extant example of native incunabula. His age at the time of his decease was about seventy-five, as in two depositions made in April, 1656, and recently reproduced by Dr. Green, he calls himself then sixty-two years old, so that, in all probability, he was born in 1594. The house in which Daye died was at the southwestern corner of Massachusetts Avenue and Dunster Street (Harvard Square), in Cambridge. About twenty years ago a stone tablet bearing the following inscription was placed in the eastern wall of the building:

HERE LIVED

STEPHEN DAYE
FIRST PRINTER IN
BRITISH AMERICA
1638–1668

In September, 1667, soon after the death of John Wilson, John Davenport was called from New Haven to the First Church in Boston, where he preached from 1666 until his death in March, 1670. In 1669 he published a catechism for the use of his new congregation, which was printed by Green, but is not now known. Our knowledge of the former existence of this edition is based on the following extract, copied from the appendix to the "Cambridge Platform," reprinted in Boston in 1701 for the First Church in Boston, and edited by James Allen, who had been Davenport's colleague: "The Reverend Mr. John Davenport, in his Catechism, Printed Anno 1669 for the use of the first Church in Boston, of which he was then Pastor; shows his concurrence with the Platform of Church Discipline, in matters Relating to Church Government." Green's other imprints of 1669, five in number, were all produced in connection with Johnson.

Of the thirteen publications issued by Green in 1670, eight were printed with the assistance of Johnson. Among his separate publications were the Harvard Theses at the 1670 Commencement; Oxenbridge's

"Seasonable Proposition of Propagating the Gospel
by Christian Colonies in the Continent of Guiana,"
published without a regular title-page; and Samuel
Mather's "Testimony from the Scripture against Idolatry & Superstition, in Two Sermons . . . . Preached,
Sept. 27 and 30, 1660," the title-page of which fails
to give the printer's name, date, or place of printing.
Thomas assigns the date of 1670, and mistakenly
adds "reprinted at Cambridge." This edition, however, is the original issue of the book, published from
the author's manuscript by his brother, Increase
Mather, whose reversed initials, "M. I.," are sub-
scribed to the prefatory address. Prince noted: "Mr.
B. Green tells me, This was Printed at Cambridge
by his Father's Letter, before He can Remember, He
supposes between 1672 & 1680." Dr. Green, following Thomas, places the book under 1670, which is
the probable date.

The last books printed jointly by Green and Johnson
bear date of 1671: Samuel Danforth's "Brief Recognition of New-Englands Errand into the Wilderness,"
Mitchel's "Nehemiah on the Wall in Troublesom
Times" and Eleazer Mather's "Serious Exhortation
to the Present and Succeeding Generation in New-
England." The only other work issued by Green
in 1671 was Jeremiah Shepard's "Ephemeris of the
Coelestial motions for the Year 1672," printed in the
last month of the year.

The imprints of 1673 include two sermons, an almanac, the first publication of the Plymouth Laws,
and the third revision of the Massachusetts Laws.

The finest copy of the Plymouth Laws to come upon the rare book market is Brinley's, in brown levant morocco extra, by Bedford, which brought only $130 in 1879. Brinley's copy of the Massachusetts law book of 1672, one of the chief undertakings of Green's press, was bound uniform with the Plymouth Colony Laws. It also fetched but $130, a sum far under the present value of the book. The best example of the book with which we are acquainted is the Lefferts copy, "clear, crisp, and crackling, in the original sheep," which realized £105 in London in 1903. This is rivalled by the copy in the Boston Athenaeum Library, which contains a long series of the supplements which were issued until the overthrow of the Colonial Government and the termination of the First Charter, May 20, 1686. It was owned and completed by Elisha Hutchinson, the grandfather of Governor Thomas Hutchinson.

In 1673 Green issued the first edition of the Colony Laws of Connecticut, the lost third edition of Wigglesworth's "Day of Doom," a broadside, four volumes of sermons, and an almanac for 1674. The Connecticut law book, the first printed edition of the colony's laws, is one of the rarest and most valuable issues of the Cambridge press. The Brinley copy, which sold for $300 in 1879, is probably the only one offered at public sale for over a century. This fine example is now owned by the state of Connecticut, and is in the state library in Hartford. Another perfect copy is in the Public Record Office, in London; a third, acquired in the latter part of 1902, is in the library of the

Connecticut Historical Society. Five other copies are known, but exist in imperfect state. The four religious publications of 1673 were by John Oxenbridge, Thomas Shepard, the younger, Urian Oakes, and Samuel Willard. Only one of the four need now concern us: Willard's "Useful Instructions for a Professing People in Times of great security and degeneracy. Delivered in several Sermons on Solemn Occasions." Of this exceedingly rare work, the earliest of Willard's many publications, only three copies seem to be known: Brinley's, in the Library of Congress, perfect; the Harvard University library copy, which lacks a leaf; and the perfect example in the library of Dr. Samuel A. Green. The second of the three sermons included in this volume refers to a case of supposed witchcraft in Groton, where Willard was pastor for thirteen years.

A list of Theses at the Commencement of Harvard College, a folio broadside, is among Green's publications in 1674. It gives, in four columns, the names of the graduates for the years 1642–1651, 1652–1659, 1660–1665, and 1666–1674. A copy is preserved in the London Public Record Office. The four religious publications of 1674 include James Fitch's "Holy Connexion," the earliest printed Connecticut election sermon, and the quaintly titled work of Urian Oakes (whose first published work, "New-England Pleaded with," had been printed by Green during the preceding year): "The Unconquerable all-conquering, & more-then-conquering Souldier." The almanac for 1675, printed toward the end of 1674, compiled by "J. F. [John Foster]," is interesting to collectors of early New England books on account of its being the earliest work to contain the initials of the man who, on the death of Marmaduke Johnson, became the first printer in Boston. The Brinley copy belonged to the long series of New England almanacs gathered by Judge Sewall.

During the following year, 1675, Green issued two interesting tracts by Increase Mather: "Severall Laws & Orders, etc." (a supplement to the law book of 1672); and the earliest of the two forms of one of the rarest of the accounts of the war with King Philip, which, breaking out in 1675, inspired a series of narratives upon its progress. The latter is the first edition of the account, by Captain Thomas Wheeler, of the attack by the Indians on Hutchinson's command near Brookfield: "A True narrative of the Lords Providences in various dispensations towards Capt. Edward Hutchinson of Boston and myself," etc., without place or date, but printed in Cambridge in 1675 by Samuel Green. The second edition: "Cambridge, Printed and Sold by Samuel Green 1676," is entitled, in part: "A Thankefull Remembrance of Gods Mercy To several Persons at Quabaug or Brookfield: Partly in a Collection of Providences about them, and Gracious Appearances for them: And partly in a Sermon Preached By Mr. Edward Bulkley." The first variety of Wheeler's account is wonderfully rare; several copies are known of the tract in its later form.

The establishment, in Boston in 1675, of John Foster's press, was the second show of typographical rivalry in New England. We have seen that Marmaduke Johnson died in December, 1674, his death occurring at a time when he had removed his press and types to Boston, and, by permission of the General Court in an order passed at the May session of 1674, had in all probability set up his press, and was preparing to print. Foster, aided by the encouragement of Increase Mather, seems to have purchased Johnson's press, and to have begun as a printer as early as April in 1675, although he was not a practical typographer, and had, indeed, no especial acquaintance with the art of printing. He is known to have been the earliest New England engraver, and, doubtless, as Dr. Green suggests, perhaps the natural connection between the two arts, strengthened by his own tastes, led him to take up the new calling. His first book was Increase Mather's "The Wicked Man's Portion," the preface of which is dated April 15, 1675, his second Mather's "The Times of Men are in the Hand of God," which soon followed the former, the preface bearing the date of June 9, 1675. Dr. Trumbull thought that Foster's almanac for 1676 was "probably the first production of the Boston press."

In addition to the "Thankefull Remembrance," Samuel Green printed in 1676 Willard's second published work, "The Heart Garrisoned," Sherman's almanac for 1677, and a Thanksgiving proclamation, issued in broadside form. The latter, the earliest Thanksgiving broadside extant, is a proclamation "at a Council, held at Charlestown, June the 20th, 1676," appointing June 29 as a thanksgiving after "long and Continued Series of Afflictive dispensations in & by the present Warr with the Heathen Natives of this Land." A copy is in the library of the Massachusetts Historical Society.

The year 1677 was rendered notable by the appearance of Urian Oakes's "Elegie Upon The Death of the Reverend Mr. Thomas Shepard," a poem in fifty-two six-line stanzas, remarkable for its personal interest, in which the "Particular Friend" of Thomas Shepard, the younger, "embalmed the memory of his Departed Jonathan." This elegy, which in some respects is the best poem written in the colonies before the eighteenth century, contains this excellent couplet:

> "Hee's gone alas! Down in the dust must ly
> As much of this rare person as could dy."

Another interesting imprint of 1677 is John Wilson's "Seasonable Watch-Word unto Christians against the Dreams & Dreamers of this Generation," which was printed by Samuel Green, aided by his eldest son, Samuel Green, Jun. This was probably the first work to contain the name of the younger Green, a name which, beginning with 1682, was for eight years connected with the production of many important Boston imprints.

In 1678 the elder Green printed a list of Harvard Theses, an almanac, and Increase Mather's "Pray for the Rising Generation;" in 1679, when he was engaged with the production of the second and revised edition of the Indian New Testament, which appeared a year later, his publications were only two in number, a sermon and an almanac. The Indian New Testament is apparently the only work printed in Cambridge in 1680. 1681, an equally barren year, witnessed the appearance of one Cambridge imprint, an almanac. Foster died in Dorchester on September 9 of this year, and, his Boston press passing under the supervision of Judge Sewall, the services of the younger Green seem soon to have been enlisted to attend to the printing, the first book printed by him being Willard's "Brief Animadversions."

During the eleven years following 1681 the Cambridge press was inactive to a large degree, the bulk of the printing business in the Massachusetts Colony being carried on in Boston. In 1682 appeared two editions of the earliest and one of the most authentic of the series of works known to collectors of Americana as Indian Captivities: "The Soveraignty & Goodness of God, Together with the Faithfulness of His Promise Displayed; Being a Narrative of the Captivity and Restauration of Mrs. Mary Rowland-son." No copy of the first edition is exant. In 1683 the fourth edition of Wigglesworth's "Day of Doom" is supposed to have been issued from the press of the elder Green. The almanac for 1684, printed this year, bore the new title of "Cambridge Ephemeris." An almanac was the solitary imprint of 1684, Samuel Green being still busily occupied with the printing of the second edition of the entire Indian Bible, which appeared in 1685 in a handsome volume, the typo-graphical superior of the first edition. The second edition of another Indian publication, Eliot's translation of Bayly's "Practice of Piety," also appeared in 1685. The almanac printed this year (the printing was not actually finished, however, until 1686) was called "New-England Almanac for the Year 1686." Its compiler was Samuel Danforth. The imprint reads: "Samuel Green, Sen. Printer to Harvard Colledge."

The few remaining titles of Cambridge imprints include five Indian books: "The Dying Speeches of several Indians," by John Eliot, [1686]: Eliot's "Indian Primer," [1687], a new impression, known only by an imperfect copy in the library of the Massachusetts Historical Society; Baxter's "Call to the Unconverted," second edition of Eliot's translation; Shepard's "Sincere Convert," translated by Eliot and Rawson, 1689; and Cotton's "Spiritual Milk for Babes," Rawson's translation of the catechism for children, 1691. The first of the five books is in English. It is a little volume of eight leaves, the title running lengthwise within borders on the title leaf. There is no imprint, but the volume was undoubtedly printed by Samuel Green and issued, perhaps, about 1686. The preface, signed John Eliot, is as follows: "Here be But a few of the Dying Speeches & Counsels Of such Indians as dyed in the Lord. It is an humbling to me that there be no more, it was not in my heart to gather them, but Mayor Gookins hearing some of them rehearsed, he first moved that Daniel should gather them, in the Language as they were spoken, and that I should translate them into English, and here is presented what was done that way. These

things are Prined [sic], not so much for publishment,
as to save charges of writeing out of Copyes for those
that did desire them." The Brinley copy of this
curious production, which cost the Lenox Library
$145 in 1879, was then called the only known copy,
and still holds that distinction.

The "Almanack for the Year MDCXCI. By John
Tulley" was printed by "Samuel Green and B. Green."
Samuel Green, Jun., who had printed Tulley's almanacs, 1687–1690, in Boston, died there in the latter part
of 1960. Bartholomew Green, his younger brother,
had set up in the printing business in Boston early in
1690. His shop was destroyed by fire soon after its
establishment, and he was obliged to return to Cambridge, where he assisted his father in the printing of
Tulley's almanacs for 1691 and 1692, Rawson's Indian
version of John Cotton's "Spiritual Milk for Babes,"
and Cotton Mather's "Ornaments for the Daughters
of Zion." The last page of the almanac for 1692 announces that "There may Speedily be Published a
little Book, Entitled, Ornaments for the Daughters of
Zion, Or the Character & Happiness of a Vertuous
Woman. By a Reverend Divine of Boston." This
well-known work, by Cotton Mather—the only book
by him printed in Cambridge—is extant to-day in two
issues, the first dated 1691, the second 1692. The latter
issue is scarce, but not particularly so. The first issue,
which is much rarer than most bibliographers and
collectors imagine, is now represented, to my knowl-
ledge, by one copy—Prince's—in the Boston Public
Library.

With the publication of the second issue of Mather's "Ornaments for the Daughters of Zion," most probably brought out in the early part of 1692, printing in "our Cambridge" came to an end. Ten years later, Samuel Green died at his home in Cambridge, aged eighty-seven. His final connection with American typography was his gift to his son Bartholomew Green of a printing press and types, on the latter's return to Boston in the autumn of 1692, where he re-established himself with much success, finally becoming the authorized printer of the laws of the Massachusetts Colony. With the father's retirement and the son's removal to Boston, Cambridge, which for thirty-seven years was the only town in English America which contained a printing press, was no longer our chief home of typography, slumbering typographically until the American Revolution.

Ornaments for the Daughters of Zion.

OR

The CHARACTER and HAPPINESS

Of A

Vertuous Woman:

in A

DISCOURSE

Which Directs

The FEMALE-SEX how to Express,
THE FEAR OF GOD, in every
Age and *State* of their LIFE ; and
Obtain both *Temporal* and *Eternal*
Blessedness.

Written By COTTON MATHER

Tertullian's advice for the Ornaments
of *WOMEN.*

*Prodite Vos jam Ornamentis Extructe A
postolorum.—Vestite Vos Serico Pietatis, Byssino
Sanctitatis, Purpurâ Pudicitie—Deum ha-
bebitis Amatorem.* In English.

Go yee forth now array'd with such *Ornaments* as the *Apostles* have provided for
you ; Cloath your selves with the *Silk* of
Piety, the *Satin* of Sanctity, the *Purple* of
Modesty ; So the Almighty God will be
a *Lover* of you.

CAMBRIDGE : Printed by S. G. &
B. G. for Samuel Phillips at Boston. 1692.

Ornaments for the Daughters of Zion. 1692

A BIBLIOGRAPHICAL LIST OF THE ISSUES OF THE CAMBRIDGE PRESS

1638 (?)

[The Freeman's Oath. Cambridge, Stephen Daye, 1638.]

> Broadside. No copy is now extant. The earliest contemporary reprint is in Vassall's "New England's Jonas Cast up at London," London, 1647.

1638 (?)

[An Almanack for the Year 1639. By William Peirce. Cambridge, Stephen Daye, 1639.]

> No copy is known.

1640

The Whole Booke of Psalmes, Faithfully Translated into English Metre. [By Richard Mather, John Eliot, and Thomas Welde. Cambridge, Stephen Daye,] 1640.

> First edition of "The Bay Psalm Book," and the earliest extant production of the Cambridge Press. Ten copies are known, six of which are imperfect.
>
> Perfect copies: (1) In Bodleian Library (Tanner copy); (2) In John Carter Brown Library (Mather-Prince copy); (3) In New York Public Library (Lenox collection); (4) In Cornelius Vanderbilt Library (Prince-Crowninshield-Brinley copy).
>
> Imperfect copies: (1) In American Antiquarian Society Library (Thomas copy); (2) and (3) in Boston Public Library (Prince copies); (4) In E. Dwight Church Library (Hurst copy); (5) In Harvard University Library (Cooke copy); (6) In A. T. White Library (Prince-Livermore copy).

1642 (?)

[A List of Theses at the Commencement of Harvard College. Cambridge, Stephen Daye, 1642.]

Broadside. No copy is known. It is given, however, in "New England's First Fruits," London, 1643, from the original: "printed in Cambridge in New-England."

1643 (?)

[Capital Laws of Massachusetts Bay. Cambridge, Stephen Daye, 1643.]

This is the "Body of Liberties," the first Code, prepared by Nathaniel Ward. The Cambridge edition is referred to in the preface of "New England's Jonas," London, 1647; but no copy is extant.

1643

A List of Theses at the Commencement of Harvard College. Cambridge, [Stephen Daye,] 1643.

Broadside. The second extant production of the press. The library of the Massachusetts Historical Society contains the only known copy, which is imperfect.

1644 (?)

[Spelling Book. Cambridge, Stephen Daye, 1646.]

No copy is now in existence.

1645 (?)

[An Almanack for the Year 1646. By Samuel Danforth. Cambridge, Stephen Daye, 1646].

Now represented by one copy (imperfect at the beginning and the end), once in the Brinley collection, next in the possession of John Boyd Thacher, of Albany, N. Y., and now owned by Mr. E. Dwight Church, of Brooklyn, N. Y.

146

1645 (?)

A Declaration of Former Passages and Proceedings Betwixt the English and the Narrowgansets. [Cambridge, Stephen Daye,] 1645.

There is a copy in the Massachusetts Historical Society Library, another is in the New York Public Library (Lenox collection), a third is in the collection of Robert Hoe, of New York City, and a fourth is in a private library in Boston. Dr. Green says that "four copies are known to be in existence."

1646 (?)

An Almanack for the Year 1647. By Samuel Danforth. Cambridge, Matthew Day, 1647.

The only work which bears the imprint of the second printer in English America. The Brinley copy, purchased by John Boyd Thacher, and now owned by E. Dwight Church, is probably unique.

1647 (?)

An Almanack for the Year 1648. By Samuel Danforth. Cambridge, [Matthew Day,] 1648.

The Brinley-Thacher-Church copy is considered unique.

1647

[A List of Theses at the Commencement of Harvard College.] Cambridge, [Matthew Day,] 1647.

Broadside. The only known copy (lacking the upper half) is in the library of the Massachusetts Historical Society.

1647

The Whole Booke of Psalmes. [Cambridge, Matthew Day,] 1647.

The second edition of "The Bay Psalm Book." Two copies are known—one in the British Museum, one in the John Carter Brown Library.

147

1648 (?)

[Book of Laws and Liberties. Cambridge, Matthew Day, 1648.]

No copy is known. It was not published, in all probability, until 1649.

1648 (?)

[Salem Catechism. By Edward Norris. Cambridge, Matthew Day, 1648.]

Supposed to have been issued after the law book, but no copy is extant.

1648 (?)

An Almanack for the Year 1649. By Samuel Danforth. Cambridge, [Samuel Green,] 1649.

Probably the first work printed by Samuel Green, the third printer at the press. The Brinley copy, now in the New York Public Library (Lenox collection), is thought to be unique.

1649 (?)

An Almanack for the Year 1650. [By Urian Oakes.] Cambridge, Samuel Green, 1650.

The Brinley copy, purchased by Mr. Thacher, and now in Mr. Church's collection, is considered unique.

1649

A Platform of Church Discipline. [By Richard Mather], Cambridge, S G, 1649.

The first edition of the "Cambridge Platform," and the earliest work bearing the imprint of the third Cambridge printer. Copies are in the New York Public Library (Lenox collection); Boston

Public Library (Brinley-Ives copy); American Antiquarian Society
Library (Increase Mather's copy), E. Dwight Church collection,
&c.

1650 (?)

[Roxbury Catechism. By Samuel Danforth. Cambridge, Samuel Green, 1650.]

Printed by Green between the "Sinod Books" (the "Cambridge Platform") and "The Bay Psalm Book" of 1651. No copy is known.

1650 (?)

[Several Laws and Orders. Cambridge, Samuel Green, 1650.]

Supplement to the law book of 1648–49. No copy is known.

1651

The Psalmes Hymns and Spiritual Songs of the Old and New Testament, faithfully translated into English metre. [By Henry Dunster and Richard Lyon.] Cambridg, Samuel Green, 1651.

The first edition of the revised version of "The Bay Psalm Book." The Kalbfleisch copy, now in the New York Public Library (Lenox collection), is probably unique.

1652

The Summe of Certain Sermons upon Genes: 15. 6. By Richard Mather. Cambridg, Samuel Green, 1652.

The first work of Richard Mather printed in New England over his name, with the possible exception of a catechism which is said to have been issued, but which is not now extant. Only a few perfect copies are in existence.

149

1654 (?)

[Indian Primer or Catechism. By John Eliot. Cambridge, Samuel Green, 1654.]

Eliot's short catechism, the earliest printed book in the Massachusetts Indian language of which any record has been found. No copy is known.

1654 (?)

[Several Laws and Orders. Cambridge, Samuel Green, 1654.]

The second supplement to the Code of 1648–49. No copy is known.

1655 (?)

An Almanack for the Year 1656. By T. S. Cambridg, Samuel Green, 1656.

There is a copy in the library of the American Antiquarian Society.

1655 (?)

[The Book of Genesis. Translated into the Massachusetts Indian Language by John Eliot. Cambridge, Samuel Green, 1655.]

Eliot's second publication in the Indian language. No copy is known.

1655

Gods Mercy, shewed to his People in giving them a faithful Ministry and Schooles of Learning for the continual supplyes thereof. By Charles Chauncey. Cambridg, Samuel Green, 1655.

Only a few copies seem to be known. Brinley's copy is in the New York Public Library (Lenox collection).

1655 (?)

[The Gospel of Matthew. Translated into the Massachusetts Indian Language by John Eliot. Cambridge, Samuel Green, 1655.]

Eliot's third publication in the Indian language. No copy is known.

1656 (?)

An Almanack for the Year 1657. By S. B. [Samuel Brackenbury.] Cambridg, Samuel Green, 1657.

By the compiler of the almanac for 1667, which gives his name in full. A copy is in the library of the American Antiquarian Society.

1656

Spiritual Milk for Boston Babes in either England. By John Cotton. Cambridg, S. G. 1656.

A single copy is extant — the Livermore example, in the New York Public Library (Lenox collection).

1657

A Farewell Exhortation to the Church and People of Dorchester. By Richard Mather. Cambridge, Samuel Green, 1657.

This is one of the rarest of the Cambridge imprints. Even Brinley could not find a good copy.

1657 (?)

[Several Laws and Orders. Cambridge Samuel Green, 1657.]

The third supplement to the Code of 1648–49. No copy is known.

1657 (?)

Verses Made by John Wilson, Pastor to the first Church in Boston; on the sudden Death of Mr. Joseph Brisco. [Cambridge, Samuel Green, 1657.]

Broadside, with black border. Printed soon after Brisco's death, January 1, 1657. A copy is in the collection of Dr. S. A. Green.

1657

The Watering of the Olive Plant in Christs Garden. A Short Catechism for the first Entrance of our Chelmesford Children. By John Fisk. Cambridg, Samuel Green, 1657.

By John Fiske, the first Chelmsford pastor. The Livermore copy, in the New York Public Library (Lenox collection), is probably unique.

1658 (?)

An Almanack for this present Year 1659. By Zech: Brigden. Cambridg, Samuel Green, 1659.

Brinley's copy is in the Library of Congress.

1658 (?)

[A few Psalms in Metre. Translated into the Massachusetts Indian Language by John Eliot. Cambridge, Samuel Green, 1658.]

This little book is referred to in Eliot's letter to Richard Floyd, dated December, 28, 1658, as one of the three portions of Scripture which had been printed: "Genesis, and Matthew, and a few Psalmes in Meeter." No copy has been found.

152

1659 (?)

An Almanack for the Year 1660. By S. C. [Samuel Cheever.] Cambridg, Samuel Green, 1660.

> The Brinley copy is in the Library of Congress.

1659 (?)

[A Declaration of the General Court of the Massachusetts Holden at Boston in New England October 18, 1659. Concerning the Execution of two Quakers. Cambridge, Samuel Green, 1659.]

> Broadside. No copy is known. It was reprinted in London the same year.

1659

The Heart of N–England rent at the Blasphemies of the Present Generation. Or a brief Tractate concerning the Doctrine of the Quakers. By John Norton. Cambridg, Samuel Green, 1659.

> One of the rarest of the early Cambridge books.

1659

An Humble Proposal for the Inlargement of University of Learning in New England. [Cambridge, Samuel Green,] 1659.

> Broadside. A copy is in the Massachusetts Archives.

1659

Some Helps for the Indians. By Abraham Peirson. Cambridg, Samuel Green, 1658.

> In the Connecticut dialect. The third Indian catechism, actually printed during the fall or early winter of 1659. The New York Public Library (Lenox collection) copy is unique. The British Museum has the only known copy of another issue, containing an altered title-page, which was probably substituted in England.

153

1660 (?)

An Almanack for the Year 1661. By S. C. [Samuel
Cheever.] Cambridg, S. G. and M. I., 1661.

> The Brinley copy is in the Library of Congress.

1660

The Book of the General Lawes and Libertyes.
Cambridge, [Samuel Green,] 1660.

> The last book printed solely by Green before the coming of the
> fourth Cambridge printer, Marmaduke Johnson. Perfect copies
> are in the American Antiquarian Society Library, Boston Athe-
> aeum Library, New York Public Library (Lenox collection),
> Pennsylvania Historical Society Library, and the State House,
> Massachusetts.

1660

A Brief Catechisme Containing the Doctrine of Godlines. By John Norton. Cambridg, S. G. and M.
J., 1660.

> Norton's lesser catechism, printed during his Boston ministry,
> for the use of the children of his congregation. The Livermore
> copy is in the New York Public Library (Lenox collection); the
> copy in the library of the Massachusetts Historical Society lacks
> the title-page. No others seem to be known.

1660 (?)

[A Christian Covenanting Canfession. Cambridge,
Samuel Green, 1660.]

> Quarto broadside, printed in two columns, in Massachusetts
> Indian and English. Only one copy is known, the one in the
> library of the University of Edinburgh.

154

1661 (?)

An Almanack for the Year 1662. By Nathaniel Chauncy. Cambridg, Samuel Green, 1662.

> The Brinley copy is in the Library of Congress; the American Antiquarian Society copy lacks the title-page.

1661

The New Testament, translated into the Indian language. [By John Eliot.] Cambridge: Samuel Green and Marmaduke Johnson, MDCLXI.

> First edition of the Indian New Testament.

1661 (?)

[A Short Catechism. By James Noyes. Cambridge, Samuel Green, 1661.]

> Title from the addenda to Haven's list. No copy is known.

1662 (?)

An Almanack for the Year 1663. By Israel Chauncy. Cambridge: S. Green and M. Johnson, 1663.

> A copy is in the library of the American Antiquarian Society; another—Brinley's—is in the Library of Congress.

1662 (?)

[The Day of Doom. By Michael Wigglesworth. Cambridge, Samuel Green and Marmaduke Johnson, 1662.]

> The first edition of this poem, no copy of which is known.

155

1662 (?)

[Indian Primer or Catechism. By John Eliot. Cambridge, Samuel Green and Marmaduke Johnson, 1662.]

> Second edition of Eliot's short catechism. No copy is known.

1662

Propositions concerning the Subject of Baptism and Consociation of Churches. [By Jonathan Mitchel.] Cambridge, S. G., 1662.

> Cotton Mather says in the "Magnalia" that the pamphlet was "chiefly of his (Mitchel's) composure."

1663 (?)

An Almanack for the Year 1664. By Israel Chauncy. Cambridge S. Green and M. Johnson, 1664.

> There is a copy, lacking one leaf, in the library of the American Antiquarian Society.

1663

A Brief Summe of the cheif articles of our Christian Faith, Composed in way of Question and Answer, Now Published, especially for the Benefit of the Town of Hampton. [By Seaborn Cotton.] Cambridge, Samuel Green, 1663.

> By John Cotton's eldest son, who began to preach at Hampton, then in Massachusetts, now in New Hampshire. For a long time no copy was thought to be extant. The Livermore copy, now in the New York Public Library (Lenox collection), is considered unique.

156

1663

Another Essay for the Investigation of the Truth.
By John Davenport. Cambridge, Samuel Green
and Marmaduke Johnson, 1663.

1663

The Cause of God and his People in New-England.
By John Higginson. Cambridg, Samuel Green,
1663.

The earliest printed Massachusetts election sermon.

1663

The Church-Membership of Children and their Right
to Baptisme. By Thomas Shepard. Cambridg,
Samuel Green, 1663.

1663

A Discourse about Civil Government in a New Plantation whose Design is Religion. By John Cotton.
Cambridge: Samuel Green and Marmaduke Johnson, MDCLXIII.

Really written by John Davenport.

1663

The Holy Bible. Translated into the Indian Language
[by John Eliot.] Cambridge: Samuel Green and
Marmaduke Johnson, MDCLXIII.

The first edition of the entire Indian Bible.

1663

[Metrical Psalms. Translated into the Indian Language by John Eliot. Cambridge, Samuel Green and Marmaduke Johnson, 1663.]

Separately issued, probably with special title. No copies seem to be extant.

1663

[Psalter or Book of Psalms. Translated into the Indian Language by John Eliot. Cambridge, Samuel Green and Marmaduke Johnson, 1663.]

500 extra copies appear to have been struck off and separately bound. No copies are known to exist.

1663

Severall Laws and Orders Made at the Severall General Courts in the Years 1661. 1662. 1663. Cambridge, Samuel Green, 1663.

Issued as a supplement to the Book of General Laws of 1660.

1664 (?)

An Almanack for the Year 1665. By Alex. Nowell. Cambridge: Samuel Green, 1665.

1664

Animadversions upon the Antisynodalia Americana. By John Allin. Cambridge: S. G. and M. J. 1664.

1664 (?)

[The Assembly's Shorter Catechism. Translated by John Eliot into the Indian Language. Cambridge, Samuel Green and Marmaduke Johnson, 1664.]

Mentioned in "The Present State of New-England," London, 1675, as having been translated by Eliot and printed in the Indian language. No copy has been found.

1664 (?)

[Call to the Unconverted. By Richard Baxter. Translated into the Indian Language by John Eliot. Cambridge, Samuel Green and Marmaduke Johnson, 1664.]

1000 copies were printed, but the entire edition has disappeared.

1664 (?)

The Conditions for New Planters in the Territories of His Royal Highnes the Duke of York. [Cambridge, Samuel Green, 1664.]

Broadside. A copy is in the Massachusetts Historical Society Library.

1664

A Defence of the Answer and Arguments of the Synod met at Boston in the Year 1662. [By Richard Mather.] Together with an Answer [by Jonathan Mitchel] to the Apologetical Preface set before that Essay. Cambridge, S. Green and M. Johnson, 1664.

Copies of this important work are in the American Antiquarian Society Library, Boston Public Library (Prince's), and New York Public Library (Lenox collection). The latter, once Brinley's, was presented by Mather to Thomas Shepard.

1664

A Discourse of the Last Judgement. By Samuel Whiting. Cambridge, S. G. and M. J., 1664.

1664

Severall Laws and Orders. Cambridge, Samuel Green, 1664.

> Issued as a supplement to the law book of 1660.

1664 (?)

[The Sincere Convert. By Thomas Shepard. Cambridge, Samuel Green and Marmaduke Johnson, 1664.]

> The first edition was printed in London in 1641. The American Antiquarian Society's copy of the Cambridge edition lacks the title-page.

1664

Three Choice and Profitable Sermons Upon Severall Texts of Scripture. By John Norton. Cambridge: S. G. and M. I., 1664.

1665 (?)

An Almanack for the Year 1666. By Josiah Flint. Cambridge: [Samuel Green] 1666.

1665 (?)

[The Assembly's Shorter Catechism. Cambridge, Samuel Green, 1665.]

> Title taken from the addenda to Haven's list. No copy has been traced.

1665

An Astronomical Description of the late Comet or Blazing Star. By S. D. [Samuel Danforth.] Cambridge, Samuel Green, 1665.

160

1665

Communion of Churches. By John Eliot. Cambridge: Marmaduke Johnson. 1665.

> The first privately printed book issued in English America.

1665 (?)

A Direction for a Publick Profession in the Church Assembly. [By John Higginson. Cambridge, Samuel Green, 1665.]

> No regular title-page.

1665 (?)

[Dorchester Catechism. By Richard Mather. Cambridge, Samuel Green, 1665.]

> A "new impression" of Mr. Mather's "Catechismes" was voted for in 1665, and apparently printed; but has vanished.

1665 (?)

A Funeral Elegie On the Death of the Memorable and truly Honourable John Winthrope Esq. [By Percival Lowell. Cambridge, Samuel Green, 1665.]

> Quarto broadside. Two columns in verse, signed "Perciful Lowle." A copy is in the Robert C. Winthrop collection.

1665

Practice of Piety. [By Lewis Bayly. Translated by John Eliot into the Indian Language.] Cambridge: [Samuel Green,] 1665.

> First edition of Eliot's Indian translation. The only extant copies are probably those in the American Antiquarian Society, Bodleian, and Yale collections, the latter being the Brinley copy.

1666

Abraham's Humble Intercession for Sodom and the Lord's gracious Concessions in Answer thereunto. By Samuel Whiting. Cambridge, [Samuel Green,] 1666.

> A copy is in the John Carter Brown Library.

1666 (?)

An Almanack for the Year 1667. By Samuel Brackenbury. Cambridge, Samuel Green, 1667.

1666 (?)

[A Brief Catechism. By John Norton. Cambridge, Samuel Green and Marmaduke Johnson, 1666.]

> According to Prince's manuscript catalogue, this catechism, first printed in 1660, was again issued in 1666. No copy is known.

1666 (?)

[The Day of Doom. By Michael Wigglesworth. Cambridge, Samuel Green and Marmaduke Johnson, 1666.]

> The second edition, which has shared the fate of the first edition. An imperfect copy is in the possession of the Massachusetts Historical Society.

1666

The Indian Grammar begun. By John Eliot. Cambridge: Marmaduke Johnson. 1666.

> Mr. Eames refers to the American Philoscphical Society, Bodleian, British Museum, John Carter Brown, Edinburgh University, Göttingen University, New York Public Library (Lenox collection), Dr. Moore, and Dr. Trumbull copies.

1667 (?)

An Almanack for the Year 1668. By Joseph Dudley.
Cambridge, Samuel Green, 1668.

1667

[Proposal for Contributions to be made for the support of his Majesties Fleet in the Caribdee Islands.
Cambridge, Samuel Green, 1667.]

Broadside. A copy is preserved at the Massachusetts State
House.

1668 (?)

An Almanack for the Year 1669. By J. B. [Joseph
Browne.] Cambridge, S. G. and M. J., 1669.

1668 (?)

[Appendix of Catechism, Touching Church Government. By John Fiske. Cambridge, Samuel Green,
1668.]

Title taken from the addenda to Haven's list. No copy is known.

1668 (?)

[The Assembly's Shorter Catechism. Cambridge,
Samuel Green. 1668.]

On September 3, 1668, Green declared before the Council in
Boston that he had lately printed "the Assembly of Divines
Chatchise." No copy is known. Five other works mentioned
in his statement have also disappeared; a sixth work, "A Narration of the Plague and Fire at London," is evidently the same as
"God's Terrible Voice in the City of London," which was really
printed by Johnson.

163

1668 (?)

[A Drop of Honey. By Thomas Wilcox. Cambridge, Samuel Green, 1668.]

Another of the "lost" books.

1668

God's Terrible Voice in the City of London. By T. V. Cambridge, Marmaduke Johnson, 1668.

A copy is in the library of the American Antiquarian Society.

1668 (?)

[Isle of Pines. By Henry Nevile. Cambridge, Marmaduke Johnson, 1668.]

One of the six books printed by Johnson about 1668, four of which are lost.

1668 (?)

[Meditations on Death and Eternity. Cambridge, Marmaduke Johnson, 1668.]

Perhaps "Daily Meditations," by Philip Pain. This is another of the "lost" books.

1668 (?)

[Primer. Cambridge, Marmaduke Johnson, 1668.]

Another of the "lost" books.

1668 (?)

[The Psalms, Hymns, and Spiritual Songs of the Old and New Testament. Cambridge, Marmaduke Johnson, 1668.]

Another of the "lost" books.

1668 (?)

[Righteous Man's Evidence for Heaven. By Timothy
Rogers. Cambridge, Marmaduke Johnson, 1668.]

Another of the "lost" books.

1668

The Rise, Spring, and Foundation of Anabaptists or
Re-Baptized of our Time. Written in French by
Guy de Brez 1565 and Translated by J. S. [Joshua
Scottow]. Cambridge: Marmaduke Johnson, 1668.

The American Antiquarian Society and Massachusetts Historical
Society copies seem to be the only ones extant.

1668 (?)

[Rule of the New Creature. Cambridge, Samuel
Green, 1668.]

Another of the "lost" books.

1668 (?)

[Spiritual Milk for Babes. By John Cotton. Cambridge, Samuel Green, 1668.]

Title taken from the addenda to Haven's list. No copy is known.

1668 (?)

[Tidings from Rome. Cambridge, Samuel Green, 1668.
Another of the "lost" books.

1668

To the Elders and Ministers of every Town within
the Jurisdiction of the Massachusets in New-
England. [Cambridge, Marmaduke Johnson,] 1668.

Broadside. A copy is in the Massachusetts Historical Society
Library.

165

1668 (?)

[The Way to a Blessed Estate in this Life. Cambridge, Samuel Green, 1668.]

Another of the "lost" books.

1668

Wine for Gospel Wantons, or Cautions against Spirituall Drunkenness. By Thomas Shepard. Cambridge, [Samuel Green,] 1668.

A copy is in the American Antiquarian Society Library.

1668 (?)

[The Young Man's Monitor. Cambridge, Samuel Green, 1668.]

Another of the "lost" books.

1669 (?)

An Almanack for the Year 1670. By J. R. Cambridge: S. G. and M. J., 1670.

A copy is in the American Antiquarian Society Library.

1669

Balm in Gilead to heal Sions Wounds. By Thomas Walley. Cambridge: S. G. and M. J., 1669.

Copies are in the Boston Public (Prince collection) and Massachusetts Historical Society libraries. A second impression appeared in 1670.

1669 (?)

[Boston Catechism. By John Davenport. Cambridge, Samuel Green, 1669.]

The appendix to the "Cambridge Platform," Boston, 1701, says that this catechism was "Printed Anno 1669 for the use of the

166

first Church in Boston," of which Davenport was then pastor. No copy is known.

1669

God's Call to His People To Turn unto Him. By John Davenport. Cambridge, S. G. and M. J., 1669.

1669

The Indian Primer. Composed by J. E. [John Eliot.] Cambridge, Marmaduke Johnson, 1669.

In the Massachusetts Indian language. It contains a large and a short catechism. The only copy known is in the library of the University of Edinburgh.

1669

New-Englands Memoriall. By Nathaniel Morton. Cambridge, S. G. and M. J., 1669.

The first important work, not wholly religious in character, which was issued in English America.

1669

A True and Exact Relation of the Late Prodigious Earthquake & Eruption of Mount Etna. By the Earl of Winchilsea. Cambridge: S. G. and M. J., 1669.

A copy is in the American Antiquarian Society Library.

1670 (?)

An Almanack for the Year 1671. By D. R. [Daniel Russell.] Cambridge: S. G. and M. J., 1671.

1670

Balm in Gilead. By Thomas Walley. Cambridge: S. G. and M. J., 1670.

Second impression. On the last page appears an advertisement of Wigglesworth's "Meat out of the Eater," which was "now going to the press," but which, although printed, is not extant in this (the first) edition.

1670 (?)

A Christian Covenanting Confession. [Cambridge, Samuel Green, 1670.]

Apparently a later impression, with several alterations, of the edition of 1660 (?). The only known copy is in the Congregational Library, Boston.

1670

At a Council held at Boston Septemb. 8 1670. Cambridge, Samuel Green, 1670.

Broadside. The earliest printed proclamation of a fast day in New England known to be extant. A copy preserved at the Massachusetts State House is believed to be unique.

1670

Daily Meditations. By Philip Pain. Cambridge: S. G. and M. J., 1670.

This is possibly the same as "Meditations on Death and Eternity," mentioned in a list of six works thought to have been printed about 1668 by Johnson. A copy of the 1670 edition is in the possession of the Massachusetts Historical Society.

1670

The Life and Death of Mr. Richard Mather. By Increase Mather. Cambridge: S. G. and M. J., 1670.

> The second of Increase Mather's acknowledged publications, and "the first of his works printed in New England." Copies are in the American Antiquarian Society and Massachusetts Historical Society libraries, and in several private collections.

1670

[A List of Theses at the Commencement of Harvard College.] Cambridge, [Samuel Green,] M.DC.LXX.

> Broadside. A copy is in the possession of the Massachusetts Historical Society.

1670 (?)

[Meat out of the Eater. By Michael Wigglesworth. Cambridge, Samuel Green and Marmaduke Johnson, 1670.]

> The first edition, which has disappeared.

1670

New England's True Interest not to Lie. By W. Stoughton. Cambridge: S. G. and M. J., 1670.

> A second edition, printed later in 1670, contains the oft-quoted line: "God sifted a whole Nation that he might send choice Grain over into this Wilderness."

1670

A Quickening Word for the Hastening a Sluggish Soul to a seasonable Answer to the Divine Call.

[By John Oxenbridge.] Cambridge, S. G. and
M. J., 1670.

1670 (?)

A Seasonable Proposition of Propagating the Gospel
by Christian Colonies in the Continent of Guiana.
By John Oxenbridge. [Cambridge, Samuel Green,
1670.]

No regular title-page.

1670

A Sermon Preach'd at the Election of the Governor,
at Boston in New-England, May 19th, 1669. By
John Davenport. [Cambridge, Samuel Green and
Marmaduke Johnson], 1670.

1670 (?)

A Testimony from the Scriptures against Idolatry &
Superstition. By Samuel Mather. [Cambridge,
Samuel Green, 1670.]

1671

A Brief Recognition of New-Englands Errand into
the Wilderness. By Samuel Danforth. Cambridge:
S. G. and M. J., 1671.

1671 (?)

An Ephemeris for the Year 1672. By Jeremiah Shepard. Cambridge: Samuel Green, 1672.

$$1671$$

Indian Dialogues. By John Eliot. Cambridge, M. J., 1671.

> In English. Copies are in the Bodleian Library and New York Public Library (Lenox collection).

$$1671$$

Nehemiah on the Wall in Troublesom Times. By Jonathan Mitchell. Cambridge: S. G. and M. J., 1671.

$$1671$$

A Platform of Church-Discipline. Cambridge, Marmaduke Johnson, 1671.

> Second American edition of the "Cambridge Platform."

$$1671$$

A Serious Exhortation to the Present and Succeeding Generation in New-England. By Eleazar Mather. Cambridge, S. G. and M. J., 1671.

> The first edition. The second edition, printed by John Foster, appeared in Boston in 1678.

$$1672\ (?)$$

An Almanack for the Year 1673. By N. H. [Nehemiah Hobart.] Cambridge: Samuel Green, 1673.

$$1672$$

The Book of the General Laws of the Inhabitants of the Jurisdiction of New-Plimouth. Cambridge: Samuel Green, 1672.

1672

The General Laws and Liberties of the Massachusetts Colony: Revised & Re-printed. Cambridge,
Samuel Green, 1672.

> The second publication of the Book of General Laws.

1672

The Logick Primer. Composed by J. E. [John Eliot.]
Cambridge, M. J., 1672.

> In Indian and English. The only known copy is in the British
> Museum.

1672

Peace, the End of the Perfect and Uprigh. By James
Fitch. Cambridge: Samuel Green, 1672.

1672

The Spouse of Christ Coming out of affliction leaning
upon Her Beloved. By John Allin. Cambridge:
Samuel Green, 1672.

1673 (?)

An Almanack for the Year 1674. By J. S. [John
Sherman.] Cambridge: Samuel Green, 1674.

1673

The Book of the General Laws For the People within the Jurisdiction of Connecticut. Cambridge:
Samuel Green, 1673.

> The first edition of the Connecticut Laws.

172

1673 (?)

[The Day of Doom. By Michael Wigglesworth.
Cambridge, Samuel Green, 1673.]

The third edition. No copy is known.

1673

Eye Salve, or a Watch-Word From our Lord Iesus
Christ unto his Churches. By Thomas Shepard.
Cambridge, Samuel Green, 1673.

1673

New-England Freemen Warned and Warmed to be
Free indeed. By J. O. [John Oxenbridge.] Cambridge, Samuel Green, 1673.

1673

New-England Pleaded with, And pressed to consider
the things which concern her Peace. By Urian
Oakes. Cambridge, Samuel Green, 1673.

1673

Old Mr. Dod's Sayings; or, A Posie gathered out of
Mr. Dod's Garden. Collected by R. T. Cambridge,
Marmaduke Johnson, 1673.

1673

[Order of the Deputy-Governor and Magistrates concerning the late Awful Hand of God, consuming
our Castle by Fire. Cambridge, Samuel Green,]
1673.

Broadside. A copy is preserved at the Massachusetts State
House. Dated Boston, March 22, 1673.

1673

Useful Instructions for a Professing People in Times of great securing and degeneracy. By Samuel Willard. Cambridge, Samuel Green, 1673.

The earliest and rarest of Willard's many publications.

1673

Wo to Drunkards. By Increase Mather. Cambridge, Marmaduke Johnson, 1673.

1673

A Young Man's legacy to the Rising Generation. By Samuel Wakeman. Cambridge, Marmaduke Johnson, 1673.

1674 (?)

An Almanack for the Year 1675. By J. Foster. Cambridge Samuel Green, 1674.

Compiled by the first Boston printer.

1674

The Cry of Sodom Enquired Into. By S. D. [Samuel Danforth.] Cambridge, Marmaduke Johnson, 1674.

1674

David serving his Generation. By Samuel Arnold. Cambridge, Samuel Green, 1674.

1674

The Day of Trouble is Near. By Increase Mather. Cambridge: Marmaduke Johnson, 1674.

174

1674

An Exhortation unto Reformation. By Samuel Torrey. Cambridge: Marmaduke Johnson, 1674.

1674

An Holy Connexion. By James Fitch. Cambridge: Samuel Green, 1674.

> The earliest printed Connecticut election sermon.

1674

[A List of Theses at the Commencement of Harvard College.] Cambridge, [Samuel Green,] 1674.

> Broadside. A copy is in the Public Record Office, London.

1674

Souldiery Spiritualized. By Joshua Moodey. Cambridge: Samuel Green, 1674.

1674

The Unconquerable all-conquering, & more-then-conquering Souldier. By Urian Oakes. Cambridge: Samuel Green, 1674.

1675 (?)

[An Almanack for the Year 1676. By J. S. [John Sherman.] Cambridge, Samuel Green, 1675.

1675

A Discourse Concerning the Subject of Baptisme. By Increase Mather. Cambridge, Samuel Green, 1675.

1675

The First Principles of New-England, Concerning the Subject of Baptisme & Communion of Churches. By Increase Mather. Cambridge, Samuel Green, 1675.

1675

Several Laws & Orders Made at the Sessions of the General Court held at Boston the 13th of October, 1675. [Cambridge, Samuel Green, 1675.]

Issued as a supplement to the law book of 1672.

1675 (?)

A True narrative of the Lords Providences in various dispensations towards Capt. Edward Hutchinson of Boston and myself. By Capt. Thomas Wheeler. [Cambridge, Samuel Green, 1675.

The first issue of Wheeler's wonderfully rare account of the attack by the Indians on Hutchinson's command near Brookfield. A copy is in the John Carter Brown Library.

1676 (?)

An Almanack for the Year 1677. By J. S. [John Sherman.] Cambridge. S. Green, 1677.

1676

The Heart Garrisioned or, The Wisdome and Care of the Spiritual Souldier. By Samuel Willard. Cambridge, Samuel Green, 1676.

Willard's second publication.

1676

A Thankefull Remembrance of Gods Mercy To Several Persons at Quabaug or Brookfield. Partly in a

Collectionof Providences about them and Gracious Appearances for them; and partly in a Sermon Preached by Mr. Edward Bulkley, Pastor of the Church of Christ at Concord, upon a day of Thanksgiving. Cambridge, Samuel Green, 1676.

The second variety of Wheeler's account of the attack by the Indians on Hutchinson's command. The best of the two Brinley copies is in the New York Public Library (Lenox collection; other copies are in the John Carter Brown and Yale University libraries, and in several private collections.

1676

[Thanksgiving Proclamation.] Cambridge, [Samuel Green,] 1676.

Broadside. A copy is in the Massachusetts Historical Society Library.

1677 (?)

An Almanack for the Year 1678. By T. B. [Thomas Brattle.] Cambr., S. Green & S. Green [Jun.]: 1678.

1677

AnElegie upon the Death of the reverend Mr. Thomas Shepard, Late Teacher of the Church at Charlstown in New-England. [By Urian Oakes.] Cambridge, Samuel Green, 1677.

1677

Innocency'sComplaint. [By GeorgeJoy.] Cambridge, Samuel Green.] 1677.

Broadside. Two columns of poetry, signed at end of second column: "George Joy, Mariner, 1677."

1677

Righteousness Rained from Heaven. By Samuel Hooker. Pastor of the Church of Christ in Farmington. Cambridge: Samuel Green, 1677.

A copy is in the Boston Public Library.

1677

A Seasonable Watch-Word unto Christians against the Dreams & Dreamers of this Generation. By John Wilson. Cambridge: S. Green and S. Green, [Jun.] 1677.

1678 (?)

An Almanack for the Year 1679. By J. D. [John Danforth.] Cambridge, Samuel Green, 1679.

1678

[A List of Theses at the Commencement of Harvard College.] Cambridge, [Samuel Green,] 1678.

Broadside. A copy is in the Massachusetts Historical Library.

1678

Pray for the Rising Generation. By Increase Mather. Cambridge: Samuel Green, 1678.

1679 (?)

An Almanack for the Year 1680. [By John Foster.] Cambridge, Samuel Green, 1680.

1679

The Necessity of a well Experienced Souldiery. By J. R. [John Richardson.] Cambridg, Samuel Green, 1679.

1680

New Testament. Translated into the Indian Language. [By John Eliot.] Cambridge, Samuel Green, 1680.

Second and revised edition of the Indian New Testament.

1681 (?)

An Ephemeris for the Year 1682. By W. Brattle. Cambridge, Samuel Green, 1682.

1682

A Seasonable Discourse Wherein Sincerity & Delight in the Service of God is earnestly pressed upon Professors of Religion. By Urian Oakes. Cambridge, Samuel Green, 1682.

1682 (?)

[The Soveraignty & Goodness of God, Together with the Faithfulness of His Promise Displayed; Being a Narrative of the Captivity and Restauration of Mrs. Mary Rowlandson. Cambridge, Samuel Green, 1682.]

The first edition, which has disappeared. This is the rarest of all narratives of Indian captives.

1682

The Soveraignty & Goodness of God, Together with the Faithfulness of His Promise Displayed; Being a Narrative of the Captivity and Restauration of

179

Mrs. Mary Rowlandson. second addition Corrected and amended. Cambridge, Samuel Green, 1682.

Second edition. Copies are in the Boston Public Library (Prince collection) and the British Museum.

1683 (?)

Cambridge Ephemeris. For the Year 1684. By N. Russel. Cambridge: Samuel Green, 1684.

1683 (?)

[The Day of Doom. By Michael Wigglesworth. Cambridge, Samuel Green, 1683.]

No copy known. Title taken from the addenda to Haven's list.

1684 (?)

Cambridge Ephemeris. 1685. By W. Williams. "Cambridge, Printed by Samuel Green for the Year 1685."

Another issue: "Cambridge, Printed by Samuel Green for Samuel Phillips, 1685."

1685

Holy Bible. Translated into the Indian Language. [By John Eliot.] Cambridge, Samuel Green, MDCLXXXV.

Second edition of the entire Indian Bible.

1685 (?)

New-England Almanack For the Year 1686. By S. D. [Samuel Danforth.] Cambridge, Samuel Green, 1685.

The date in the imprint should be 1686. Not finished until 1686, although dated 1685.

180

1685

[Practice of Piety. By Lewis Bayly. Translated by
John Eliot into the Indian Language.] Cambridge,
[Samuel Green,] 1685.

Second edition of Eliot's translation. Copies are in the Boston
Public Library (Prince collection), British Museum, John Carter
Brown collection, and New York Public Library (Lenox collec-
tion), the latter being the Nodier-Brinley example.

1686 (?)

Cambridge Ephemeris. An Almanack for 1687. [By
W. Williams.] Cambridge, S. G., 1687.

1686 (?)

The Dying Speeches of several Indians. [By John
Eliot. Cambridge, Samuel Green, 1686.]

In English. Brinley's copy, the only one known, is in the New
York Public Library (Lenox collection).

1687 (?)

An Elegiack Verse, on the Death of the Pious
and Profound Grammarian and Rhetorician, Mr.
Elijah Corlet, Schoolmaster of Cambridge, who
Deceased Anno Aetatis 77, Feb. 24, 1687. [Cam-
bridge, Samuel Green, 1687.]

Broadside, printed in folio size, containing two columns within
mourning borders. An apparently unique copy of this interesting
poetical broadside (here described for the first time in any bibliographical account of American imprints) was sold in Boston, in the
Libbie auction rooms, on November 15, 1905.

The Rev. Nehemiah Walter, the author of this curious example
of early American poetry, was born in Cork, Ireland, and came

to this country in 1679, in his seventeenth year. He graduated at Harvard in 1684, and in 1688 was ordained as colleague to John Eliot, in Roxbury, officiating in that capacity until the death of the apostle in 1690. He married a daughter of Increase Mather, and was a member of the Harvard College Corporation for a number of years.

1687 (?)

[The Indian Primer. By John Eliot. Cambridge, Samuel Green, 1687.]

Apparently a new impression of Eliot's Indian Primer of 1669. The imperfect Prince copy in the library of the Massachusetts Historical Society seems to be unique.

1687

[A List of Theses at the Commencement of Harvard College.] Cambridge, [Samuel Green,] MDC.LXXXVII.

Broadside. A copy is in the library of Harvard University.

1688

[Call to the Unconverted. By Richard Baxter. Translated into the Indian Language by John Eliot.] Cambridge: S. G., 1688.

Second edition of Eliot's translation. Copies are in the American Antiquarian Society, Boston Public (Prince's), Harvard University, Massachusetts Historical Society, and Yale University collections.

1689

A Brief Discourse Concerning the unlawfulness of the Common Prayer Worship and of Laying the Hand on, and Kissing the Booke in Swearing. By a

182

Reverend and Learned Divine. [Increase Mather.]
Cambridge, Samuel Green, 1689.

A copy is in the library of the Massachusetts Historical Society.

1689 (?)

[The Declaration of the Gentlemen, Merchants, and
inhabitants of Boston, and the Country adjacent.
April 18, 1689. Cambridge, Samuel Green, 1689.]

No copy is known. A reprint is given in Byfield's "Account of
the Late Revolution in New England," London, 1689, filling pages
7–19, where it is printed "according to the Copy Printed in New
England by Samuel Green, 1689."

Mr. Luther S. Livingston kindly suggests this title as a possible
Cambridge imprint of 1689. There is a possibility, however, that
it was really printed in Boston by Samuel Green, the younger.

1689 (?)

Harvard's Ephemeris for 1690. By H. Newman. Cambridge, Samuel Green, 1690.

A copy is in the Massachusetts Historical Society Library.

1689

[The Sincere Convert. By Thomas Shepard. Translated into the Indian Language by John Eliot
and Grindal Rawson.] Cambridge, Samuel Green.
1689.

The last of Eliot's many publications. Copies are in the American Antiquarian Society, John Carter Brown, New York Public
Library (Lenox), and Yale University collections.

1690 (?)

An Almanack for the Year MDCXCI. By John Tulley.
Cambridge, Samuel Green and B. Green, 1691.

Samuel Green, Jun., who had printed Tulley's almanacs, 1687–1690, in Boston, died in July, 1690. The almanac for 1691 and the one for 1692 were printed in Cambridge, therefore, by his father and his younger brother, Bartholomew.

1690 (?)

Further Quaeries Upon the Present State of the New-English Affairs. Cambridge, Samuel Green, 1690.

Signed: "S. E."

1690

[An Order of the General Court for the Emission of Paper Money.] Cambridge, Samuel Green, 1690.

Broadside. A copy is preserved at the Massachusetts State House.

1690

Holwell's Predictions of Many Remarkable things, which may Probably Come to Pase, from the Year 1689. Untill the Year 1700. Written 1682. Cambridge, S. G., 1690.

1691 (?)

An Almanack for the Year MDCXII. By John Tulley. Cambridge: Samuel Green and Bartholomew Green, 1692.

1691

Ornaments for the Daughters of Zion. By Cotton Mather. Cambridge: S. G. and B. G., 1691.

First issue. The only known copy with this date is in the Prince collection, in the Boston Public Library.

1691

[Spiritual Milk for Babes. By John Cotton. Translated into the Indian Language by Grindal Rawson.] Cambridge: Samuel Green, kah Bartholomew Green. 1691.

Rawson's Indian translation of Cotton's catechism for children. Copies are in the American Antiquarian Society, Boston Athenaeum, John Carter Brown, Harvard University, New York Public Library (Lenox), Watkinson Library (Trumbull's), and Yale University collections.

1692

Ornaments for the Daughters of Zion. By Cotton Mather. Cambridge: S. G. and B. G., 1692.

Second issue. The last book printed at the Cambridge Press.

185

INDEX

188